ANGELS *and* SAINTS

ANGELS *and* SAINTS

A BIBLICAL GUIDE TO FRIENDSHIP
WITH GOD'S HOLY ONES

SCOTT HAHN

IMAGE
NEW YORK

All rights reserved.
Published in the United States by Image, an imprint of the
Crown Publishing Group, a division of Random House LLC,
a Penguin Random House Company, New York.
www.crownpublishing.com

IMAGE is a registered trademark and the "I" colophon is a
trademark of Random House LLC.

Library of Congress Cataloging-in-Publication data is
available upon request.

ISBN 978-0-307-59079-4
eBook ISBN 978-0-307-59080-0

Printed in the United States of America

Book design by Lauren Dong
Jacket design by Jean Traina
Jacket photograph: Francesco Dazzi

10 9 8 7 6 5 4

First Edition

To our beloved grandchildren, future saints:

Josephine Mirelle Hahn

Leo Gregory Reinhard

Lucy Josephine Hahn

Gabriel Kolbe Hahn

Bernadette Martha Hahn

Elizabeth Coeli Hahn

Naomi Thérèse Hahn

Veronica Margaret Hahn

CONTENTS

Contents

INTRODUCTION

THE CHURCH AND THE HOLY ONES

When people talk about "the Church," we know what they mean—or at least we think we do.

It's the parish we attend on Sundays that has really good preaching and music (or maybe not).

Or it's that big old institution that we're part of, that's kind of hard to explain, and that lets us down sometimes.

This book is about the Church we sometimes forget: the heavenly Church.

The heavenly Church is not a different Church or yet another denomination. It's the true Church, the Church in its essence—in its essential perfection. That's how we see the Church in the last chapters of the Book of Revelation: as a radiant bride, presented to Christ her groom, amid a great marriage supper. But it's not just off in the future. It's now. It's the Church where Jesus, the Blessed Mother, and all the angels and saints live today—in glory.

And we are united with them—by grace—just as they are totally invested in us—by love, to help the pilgrim Church to live on earth more and more like they do in heaven.

When I was a new Catholic, I was also a young theologian, just getting acquainted with the great tradition. Reading the theologians of centuries past, I reveled in their expositions of the Church—its four marks (one, holy, catholic, and apostolic) and its three states (militant, suffering, and triumphant). But I also noticed something strange. I noted that they rather consistently used a curious phrase to describe the Church. The Church, the old books said, is a "perfect society."

It struck me as odd because the Church that I knew—the Church that had received me as a grateful convert—seemed beautiful and even awesome but far from perfect. It had rich history, glorious art, intellectual coherence, and demonstrable apostolic succession. But it was also rocked by scandals and run by pastors with varying degrees of competence and differing levels of grouchiness. Many of its members seemed indifferent to its glories and, at best, intermittently engaged.

Yet the old theologians were plainly telling me not simply that "this is the best society you're likely to find, so grin and bear it"—but rather that "this is indeed the perfect society."

Perfect? I wasn't seeing it.

And that's the point. The essential perfection can't be seen. It's heavenly. God has shared his life with the

Church—divinized it—and divine glory is, for now, invisible to our mortal eyes.

Yet the perfect society is also the Church we know. Even the Church on earth is perfect, because it possesses all the means necessary for perfecting its members—and among those means are the holy angels and the saints.

None of us is canonizable till we get home, till we die. Until then, we look to the heavenly Church, whose members bear the four marks more vividly and truly than we do. We want to become more like them through all our days on earth. And we do that by growing in friendship with them.

There are not two churches, one earthly and one heavenly. God does not segregate his finished, heavenly elite from the multitude of ordinary schleps who warm the earthly pews. No, you and I believe in a Church that is at once heavenly and earthly. In that Church the saints are present and available to us. They are family to us. They are elder siblings, only purified of all rivalry, impatience, and irritability. They want to help us become as they are (holy). They want to help us get all the way home.

That is why God presents his Church to Christ as a bride, in the midst of a wedding feast. It's a family matter. A family affair.

This book is a celebration of that perfect society, that raucous family, the heavenly Church. We'll begin with a few introductory chapters on sanctity in general before proceeding to a number of chapters on saints in particular.

These later chapters are short meditations that focus on only one or two aspects of a saint's thought or accomplishments. There are many more saints and much more to learn, so I hope I'll inspire you to take up your own research.

This book contains not a catalog of saints, but just a tiny sampling. I tried to include a representative variety, including angels and regular folks, characters from the Old Testament and the New, lay and clergy, ancient and modern. But, as I prepare the book for press, I notice that my chosen saints tend to be those with whom I have something in common. Most are teachers, scholars, and writers. There is far greater diversity in the saintly communion than I've let on in this book. Should you decide to write your own book, I'm certain you'll have a different list.

With each chapter I've included writings by or about the saints under discussion. I tried to choose the passages that will best inspire prayer and rouse us to imitation of the virtues of that particular person. You'll find these under the heading "Ponder in Your Heart," a line I've taken from St. Luke, who said of the Queen of All Saints: "Mary kept all these things, pondering them in her heart" (Luke 2:19).

I pray that these saints will lead us all to a deeper understanding of the Church, the perfect society they share with us.

Part I

1

INCIDENT IN ASSISI: THE SCIENCE OF THE SAINTS

ASSISI REPRESENTS A KIND OF HOLLYWOOD ideal of heaven on earth. The town's buildings—its hotels and shops and restaurants—are medieval or at least look the part. Look in any direction, and the green, rolling hills look like landscapes from the old masters. You'll find few cars on the cobblestone streets, but at any moment you could find yourself in a throng of brown-robed pedestrians.

It's the town of St. Francis, the town of St. Clare, and its inhabitants are proud of the fact. They strive to keep it credibly Franciscan for the hundreds of thousands of pilgrims and tourists who visit each year. It's also the town of lesser-known saints such as Agnes of Assisi (Clare's little sister) and Gabriel of the Sorrowful Virgin, the ancient St. Rufinus and the Benedictine hermit St. Vitalis.

And it is the town of myriad angels. The centuries-old fortification is called the *Rocca San Angelo*—Holy Angel Fortress. The gem of Assisi's many churches is the Basilica of St. Mary of the Angels, which houses St. Francis's own *Portiuncula* (Little Portion) chapel.

So many angels and saints, but so little time. We had made quick trips to Assisi—my wife, Kimberly, and I—but we wanted to walk its streets again, to make a pilgrimage more intentional and familiar. We advertised a tour and were to play host to more than a hundred fellow pilgrims from the United States.

We were eager, then, to believe the doctor when he told us that our seven-year-old, Joe, would be well enough to make the trip—even though our flight left just two weeks after his emergency appendectomy. Joe was mending, the doctor said, in an exemplary fashion, and there was no sign of infection or complications.

Joe, for his part, didn't feel he needed a doctor to pronounce him ready. Irrepressible, athletic, and gifted with the strongest constitution in the family, he was always up for an adventure. And Assisi, with its maze of hills and alleyways, forts and castles, promised him episodes straight out of storybooks and Butler's *Lives of the Saints*.

In Assisi Joe—and we—got more of an adventure than he dreamed, but a different sort of adventure.

The doctor's healthy prognosis was confirmed by Joe's movement on the flight to Rome, and then on the bus through the mountains to Assisi. My son's voyage had begun, and he was the explorer, the crusader, the true pilgrim. His worried parents, of course, were on the alert for any sign of strain, and occasionally we made the obligatory but pointless admonition for the seven-year-old to relax and get some rest.

Our first day was partial and included only a few of the sites associated with the lives of the local saints. Still, it was enough to earn the whole family—and even Joe—a good night's sleep when we hit the pillows back at the hotel.

The itinerary for our second day was full, and we set out early. But this day was definitely different. Within the first hour, I noticed that Joe was wincing and stopping. By the second hour, he was stopping to double over. At first, when I asked, he protested that everything was okay, and he denied having any pain more than a walking cramp. But soon it became apparent that he couldn't go on. Kimberly actually removed our toddler, David, from our stroller, and set Joe in David's place.

It was clear, though, that this wouldn't be enough, and we asked our tour guide to summon us a taxi so we could visit a doctor. Kimberly and I divided the duties: she would stay behind in the old town with the other children; I would accompany Joe to the hospital.

KNOW PAIN, KNOW GAIN

The taxi delivered Joe and me to an unassuming and unimpressive building: *Ospedale di Assisi*. It wasn't what I had hoped to see. It wasn't what I would expect to see at a comparable tourist destination in the United States. The outside appearance didn't leave me with a strong sense of confidence. What everyone loves about Assisi—its long lingering in the Middle Ages—was not what I wanted to find in its practice of medicine.

My worries were relieved, slightly, by the kind expressions of the people inside. Yet their greetings only added a new cause for concern, as it became clear that we shared few words in common beyond our simple greetings. They said their halting *hellos* and we our pathetically accented *buon giornos*; and then, with gestures and pidgin phrases, we set about trying to communicate about Joe's medical history and current symptoms.

My anxiety levels climbed higher, higher than the Rocca San Angelo that overlooked the town. Joe was, by this time, writhing in my arms as he sat awkwardly in my lap.

The people from reception ushered us back to the x-ray room, where the technician was also just arriving. Quite obviously one of the town's firemen, he arrived still wearing uniform overcoat and galoshes. He did his work as quickly as possible on equipment that looked, to my untrained eye, at least a couple of decades old.

We then continued our pilgrim way to an examining room, to await the *dottore*. It was a mercifully brief wait till we met the doctor. And, as if in answer to my urgent prayers, he spoke adequate English.

He looked at the chart as I explained the situation— Joe's appendectomy, his "exemplary" recovery, and then our crisis. He nodded, then gently touched a couple spots on Joe's abdomen before Joe cried out from the pain.

The doctor led me into the hallway and said the words I wanted to hear: "I think your son will be fine." With his limited English, he explained that the pain was now in a "safe" place. But if it should shift to the other side, Joe would need immediate surgery. "And that would be a serious problem, not only because we'd have to operate, but because we'd have to operate *here*." His tone seemed to indicate that *here* was not the best location for surgery.

We checked into the hospital for an overnight stay. Joe, who was ordinarily voracious, had no appetite for food. A boy who rarely complained, he was now reduced to moaning and crying into his pillow.

I tried to keep him amused, making small talk, and he tried now and then to focus on a handheld video game, but the pain consumed his attention and wrung my paternal heart. Around ten p.m. I asked him, "Where's the pain now? Is it still in the same place?" And he said, "No, it's on the other side." I asked him if he was sure about that, and he said he was.

Joe had not heard my conversation with the doctor, so he didn't know the import of his words. I excused myself and hurried down to the nurses' station, where I asked a nurse to contact the doctor. I took up a piece of paper and wrote the words, "Pain on other side. Danger."

I returned to the room and waited for the doctor. Joe was writhing in agony. I tried to calm him, and gradually his moans subsided into a whimper as he fell in and out of an exhausted sleep. Not knowing when help might arrive, I turned off the lights in the room and did the only thing left for me to do.

I dropped to my knees in the most desperate prayer, imploring God's help in the most general and inarticulate way.

And I was startled by a sudden sense of presence—a vivid sense.

God was with me in that room. If you had turned on the lights and I had seen him, I wouldn't have been surprised. God was close to me in my helplessness. I had the clear sense that he was asking me: *What are you afraid of?*

I was taken aback, and I responded frankly, though interiorly: *Why would you even ask that? You know what I'm afraid of. I'm afraid of losing my son in surgery in a place that's not prepared to deal with this sort of problem. I love him, and I don't want him to die.*

And just as clearly I sensed God's reply: *Is that all?*

I couldn't have imagined this. I couldn't have made this up. It seemed to me that the all-knowing, all-seeing, all-compassionate God was belittling my concerns. But as long as he was asking, I'd answer with both barrels: *Well, no, that's not all. I'm also afraid what will happen to my wife, his mother. It would shatter her.*

Again the response came: *Is that all?*

So I kept going: *No, it's not. He has siblings. And here we are on a pilgrimage, far from home and responsible for a hundred pilgrims. Am I supposed to abandon them?*

And is that all?

It began to dawn on me that my fears that were on the surface—and that seemed obvious to me—were linked to deeper fears, more subtle fears that had to do with my family life, my personal life, my professional life, fears of failure, fears of loss, fears of humiliation. In an instant, my life appeared before me as a web of fears, cares, concerns, anxieties, and worries. Till that moment I'd never quite been aware of this.

But God had been. It became clear to me that God was not asking questions so that I could inform him of anything. He was asking so that I would have to formulate answers—and so he could show me how much my life was controlled by fear.

Into my mind came the first papal words of the man who was then the pope, Blessed John Paul II. He said to the world: "Be not afraid." He was echoing Jesus (Matthew 28:10) and so many angels (Luke 1:13, 2:10). And no one—not Jesus nor the angels nor Pope John Paul—ever said there was no reason to be afraid. They just told us to get over it, to get past the fear, and to accept the grace that God was extending to us through our trials.

It was then that Assisi lived up to its reputation for me. In an instant I realized that Joe and I were far from alone in the room. God was with me; but there with God were so many others. I knew the presence of the Blessed Virgin Mary, our guardian angels, and the saints whose footsteps I'd been following, Francis and Clare. There was Padre

Pio, and St. Therese of the Child Jesus, and St. Thomas Aquinas, and St. Josemaria Escriva—all saints who had significantly influenced my spiritual and intellectual life. *They were really there*, in the presence of God. They were there because they truly cared about Joe and me, and Kimberly and the pilgrims, and they were interceding for all of us.

As never before, I knew the truth of the Scripture: "Therefore, since we are surrounded by so great a cloud of witnesses, let us also lay aside every weight, and sin which clings so closely, and let us run with perseverance the race that is set before us, looking to Jesus the pioneer and perfecter of our faith, who for the joy that was set before him endured the cross" (Hebrews 12:1–2).

The saints, the great cloud of witnesses, were cheering us onward as we raced forward after Jesus our "pioneer," through our share in his cross.

The same chapter of the Letter to the Hebrews acknowledges the presence of "innumerable angels" with the saints, "the spirits of just men made perfect" (Hebrews 12:22–23); the angels, too, were with me in that room, praying with me, praying for my heart's intention: for Joe.

Please don't get me wrong. I'm not a man given to mystical flights, or visions, or locutions. My family and closest friends will testify that I'm not prone to euphoria. Nor do I think my experience was anything extraordinary. I believe I experienced, for a moment, a heightened sense of what is truly ordinary. This is the backdrop of our every-day life: The angels and saints are with us as witnesses, as friends, as family. We are never alone. We need never be afraid. This is a simple corollary of our salvation. It's a fact too easily forgotten.

"The Lord is at hand. Have no anxiety about anything, but in everything by prayer and supplication with thanks-giving let your requests be made known to God" (Philip-pians 4:5–6).

As I let my fears be known, I grew more aware of the saints' presence. They were, in a sense, more present than I was—more awake, more alert, more alive in God. They were like older siblings who had come to the aid of a younger one who's injured. My prayer became a conver-sation that included all of them. And, again, if you had flipped on the light and I had seen their faces, I wouldn't have been surprised.

There came a moment when I thought I could pray like this all night—but I realized that that would be selfish, and it would leave me useless to everyone at the time of Joe's surgery. I knew I should get up off the floor and get some sleep.

That was when it occurred to me: for the last two hours and forty-five minutes Joe hadn't uttered a peep—no cry-ing, no moaning, no writhing. He'd been sleeping peace-fully the whole time.

I didn't sense that a miracle had happened. I just felt

a certain peace, and I went to Our Lady, who had been there from the beginning, and I prayed a Rosary to close the night.

THE SCIENCE OF THE SAINTS

I woke around eight a.m. and noticed that Joe was still sleeping. I heard muffled voices in the hallway and recognized one as the doctor's. When he peeked in the doorway, I motioned for him to speak softly. He told me he had already put in a call to assemble a team for surgery.

I explained that the pain had shifted in the night, and that Joe was up late crying, but around midnight he stopped. I told him I had been on my knees praying at the time.

He smiled, indulgently but skeptically.

Suddenly Joe woke up, sat up, and said, "*Buon giorno!*" The night before he couldn't even sit up without help.

The doctor was visibly startled. "*Buon giorno*, Giuseppe," he said. "How are you feeling?"

Joe yawned and said, "Great." Still looking skeptical, the doctor lifted Joe's shirt and pressed on both sides.

Joe meanwhile told the doctor about how the pain had moved the night before, but then went away.

The doctor was incredulous and ordered tests. Over the next three hours, the nurses drew blood and passed it along to the lab.

Around midday, the doctor came back, scratching his head. "I'm not a religious man," he said to me. "I'm scientific. I don't believe in miracles. But when you practice medicine in Assisi, you encounter these things. Things happen that science can't explain."

And that, it occurs to me, is true science—what St. Edith Stein called "the science of the saints." And it is the subject of this book.

2

THE ONLY SAINT

THE ENGLISH WORD *SAINT* HAS ASSUMED A very precise, technical meaning. We use it to describe a man, woman, or child—always deceased, and usually long deceased—who has undergone the Church's approval process known as *canonization*. We use it to describe someone who is, the Church authoritatively assures us, with God in heaven and capable of interceding for us on earth. It takes the Church decades or even centuries to arrive at such a decision. Along the way, the candidate's life is subject to the most intensive scrutiny, examined by a variety of Vatican offices, as he or she moves from one honorific title to the next:

- *Servant of God* is a title conferred by the bishop who has jurisdiction to launch the investigative phase of the canonization process. It is the title used in the documentation presented to the Vatican Congregation for the Causes of the Saints.

- *Venerable* indicates that the Church has conducted an initial examination of the candidate's life and concluded that it is a life of "heroic virtue."

- *Blessed* is the title given when the Church has judged it "worthy of belief" that an individual is in heaven. The declaration usually comes after a miracle has been attributed to the candidate's intercession. The Church designates a feast day for the Blessed, though it is usually celebrated only by the Blessed's home diocese or religious order. The ceremony declaring someone blessed is called beatification, and it may be conducted by a bishop, though only with prior approval of the pope.

- *Saint* appears before the names of those the Church has declared, with certainty, to be in heaven. Canonization is the act by which the pope recognizes someone as a saint. In most cases, the person's intercessory power has been demonstrated by two postmortem miracles (one occurring after beatification). People on earth have gained otherwise inexplicable benefits—such as cures from disease or injury—by invoking the saint. Churches may be named after canonized saints, and their feast days may be celebrated anywhere in the world.

Such is a saint, at least to English speakers. Saints are the Church's all-stars, like St. Peter, St. John Bosco, and St. Teresa of Avila. But there is deeper meaning embedded in this concept. We should be aware of the roots of the word, and indeed how other languages treat the idea of sainthood, for English is a language that always seeks greater precision. This is why it serves so well for scientific and technical literature. Along the way, however, it can drain words of their nuance and suggestive power. In demanding a word that is exclusively descriptive of "official" saints, our language has lost much of the poetry—and potency—contained in the Latin *sanctus*, the Greek *hagios*, the Hebrew *kodesh*.

Other modern languages are not so exacting. In French, for example, we speak of *Saint Pierre* (St. Peter) and *le Saint Graal* (the Holy Grail) using the same term. The French word *Saint* means simply "holy," and it may be applied to a person, place, or thing that is generally considered sacred. What we call the Holy Bible is, in French, *la Sainte Bible*.

It's helpful for us to be sensitive to this as we approach our understanding of sainthood. As an English speaker, I may be capable of tremendous exactitude, but with such precision can come a loss of subtlety, complexity, and suggestive power.

We need to be aware that terms that are distinct for us—*sainthood*, *sanctity*, *holiness*—have been, for most of the world and through most of history, different aspects of the same term, and indeed the same thing.

Please don't think that this is just a word game or semantic quibble. It has enormous consequences for our Catholic faith. On most Sundays and every Holy Day, we English speakers go to Mass and we sing the ancient hymn we call the *Gloria*, "Glory to God in the highest . . ." It's a song we on earth learned from the holy angels at the birth of Jesus (see Luke 2:14); it has likely been part of the Church's liturgy since the first generation—and congregations still love to belt it out. In that hymn we sing to God and we profess: "You alone are the holy one!" In English it presents no conundrum, no riddle. But consider what people in other Catholic churches are singing. Those who use the Latin, for instance, sing the words *"Tu solus sanctus"*—meaning "You alone are the saint," or "You alone are a saint"—and they must sing those words even on the feasts of *Sanctus Petrus* or *Sanctus Paulus*, *Saint* Peter or *Saint* Paul!

Catholics have been doing this, moreover, for centuries without the slightest inner conflict—not a whiff of cognitive dissonance amid the incense.

What on earth, and what in heaven, can we mean by this word *sanctus*? What should we mean by *saint*? What can we mean by a characteristic that belongs *only* to God, even as we apply it lavishly to the Bible and the chalice, Peter and Paul, Padre Pio and the pope?

HOLINESS IS IN HEAVEN

It was not always so. Believers did not always feel free to apply the term *holy* to other believers.

In fact, before the coming of Christ, *holy* was a word

whose usage was bound in the most limited way. Strictly speaking, it was reserved for God alone. "There is none holy like the Lord, there is none besides thee" (1 Samuel 2:2).

Rabbi Joshua Berman notes that, in classical usage, the Hebrew word *kodesh* (holy) and its derivatives (like *kedushah*, holiness) are properly applied only to God.[1] In the Hebrew Scriptures, the word refers to God's essence. "Who is like you, O Lord, among the gods? Who is like you, majestic in holiness?" (Exodus 15:11; see also Amos 4:2).

The word is used to describe the Almighty—and then by extension to describe God's presence and the place or time of his dwelling. Thus, the tabernacle, the portable shrine used by the Israelites for sacrificial worship, was *kodesh*, as was the temple built by King Solomon (see, for example, Exodus 26:33 and 1 Kings 8:6). Within these places, the innermost sanctuaries, the "holy place" and the "holy of holies," functioned as kind of a reserve or preserve of God's presence. These were sites "set apart"—that's the literal meaning of *kodesh*. They were separated, by strong walls and vast courtyards, from the profane and polluted world. The priestly tribe, the Levites, guarded these regions, tended them, and kept them pure for the sake of God's presence. So quarantined was the holy of holies that only the high priest was allowed entry, and only once a year, on the Day of Atonement—and even then only briefly, to pray the formal prayers before fleeing for his life.

In the Hebrew Scriptures, Rabbi Berman points out, no individual human being is *kodesh*; none is "holy." The

Sabbath is made holy by God's special presence, as are the tabernacle and temple. Israel is holy because God has chosen to dwell among his chosen people, who collectively are his "holy ones." The ark of the covenant is holy because it is the place of his dwelling; the law is holy because it protects the purity of the sanctuary; even the priestly vestments are holy, because they are reserved for use in God's presence. But no man at this time is so "sanctified." No man is a "saint." Noah is a "just man" (Genesis 6:9). Moses is "a man of God" (Deuteronomy 33:1). David is a man after God's own heart (1 Samuel 13:14). There is only one instance when a human being is described as "holy." Elisha is so described in a wealthy woman's speculation—"I perceive that this is a holy man of God" (2 Kings 4:9)—but she speaks with no special authority, since she is neither the Lord nor his prophet. So the sole exception serves to prove the rule—and prove the claim we make when we sing the Gloria: *tu solus sanctus* . . . God alone is *holy*. God alone is a *saint*.

Holy indeed is God's essence, and "Holy" is his name. The Old Testament prophet Isaiah reported his vision of the heavenly throne, which John confirms in the New Testament Book of Revelation. Isaiah sees that above God "stood the seraphim . . . and one called to another and said: 'Holy, holy, holy is the Lord of hosts'" (Isaiah 6:2–3).

PROPHET SHARING

A curious thing, however, happens in the Book of the Prophet Daniel—specifically in chapter 7. Of all the great oracles of the prophets, this chapter is among the most significant for Christians, for it conveys his vision of "one like a Son of Man" who comes with the clouds and presents himself worthily before the throne of God. This "Son of Man" redeems the nations and rules them in the name of heaven.

He does not, however, rule alone. He shares his rule with God's people on earth. And here's the curious part: Daniel refers to God's people, *six times in that chapter*, as "saints" and four times as "saints of the most high." What's more, he says some astonishing things about them:

> [T]he saints of the Most High shall receive the kingdom, and possess the kingdom for ever, for ever and ever . . . And the kingdom and the dominion and the greatness of the kingdoms under the whole heaven shall be given to the people of the saints of the Most High; their kingdom shall be an everlasting kingdom, and all dominions shall serve and obey them. (Daniel 7:18, 27)

So Daniel sees a multitude of people who are holy—and even ruling the earth in God's name. This is exceptional in the Old Testament, but the context provides the reason for the exception. For Daniel presents these "saints" not within a historical narrative, but in the course of a prophecy of the Messiah. He is not describing something that is present or recounting anything from the past. He foresees a kingdom yet to come. Daniel's vision arrives during the Babylonian Captivity, six full centuries before the coming of Christ.

Daniel sees the Messiah as human and yet able to act with the power of God. He is a "Son of Man," yet he looks to the Ancient of Days as his father. The Son of Man, it seems, is also the Son of God! And, in Daniel's vision, he succeeds rather spectacularly where every would-be redeemer since Adam had failed. Revealed as a Son, he empowers others to become saints.

Indeed, when the Messiah *did* come, he called himself by the name Son of Man (see Matthew 20:28), and his people were known as saints. Thus, Daniel anticipated the day when God would share his kingdom with "the saints of the Most High."

Talk about foresight. Daniel had it in spades.

SAINTHOOD IS CONTAGIOUS

The situation of holiness changes rather drastically with the Gospels. In fact, what was exceptional in the Old Testament becomes the rule in the New Testament. Before

Jesus is even conceived, the angel tells the Blessed Virgin Mary: "the child to be born *will be called holy*" (Luke 1:35).

Look at the significance of this. How many times have we heard this during Advent and possibly passed it by? The child Jesus is called by God's name! He possesses a quality that belongs properly only to God! Yet the child will still be a *child*, a boy who goes out into the world—a boy who spends his early years in the land of Egypt, the geographic symbol not of holiness, but of profanity: the place that pious Jews associated with idolatry and slavery. In the midst of the tempest will be the stillness of the holy one.

The child Jesus grew to be a man who had little use for ceremonial taboos about "protecting" holiness. Ignoring the prohibition of labor on the Sabbath, he worked at healing, and he cited the divine prerogative as his own (John 5:16–17). Far from desecrating the Sabbath, his labors consecrated the day. It was his physical presence, his touch, like the touch of the host on your tongue, that made all around him holy. He announced he was "Lord of the Sabbath" (Luke 6:5). He made the Sabbath holy, and not vice versa. The Apostles recognized Jesus as "the Holy One of God" (John 6:69), and, interestingly enough, so did the demons (Mark 1:24).

So what's happening here? We see God drawing closer. No longer was he off in the distance. He was here in our midst. Jesus transgressed the boundaries set up to keep the "unclean" far from the "holy." In one rather remarkable run in Matthew's Gospel we see him touching a leper

(Matthew 8:2–3), a corpse (Matthew 9:24–25), and a bleeding woman (Matthew 9:20–22), all actions that, according to the Law of Moses, would defile a man and render him unfit to enter the temple or even the gates of the holy city, Jerusalem. Yet Jesus strode across these boundaries fearlessly, and, rather than contracting any "uncleanness" from wounded people, he communicated wholeness and healing to them. After all, what good is a doctor if he can't be among his patients?

This is symbolized in a powerful way by the rending of the temple veil as Jesus died.

"And the curtain of the temple was torn in two, from top to bottom" (Mark 15:38). There was now no barrier between humanity and the true "holy of holies," the place where the cherubim sing, "Holy, holy, holy." For we have access through "the new and living way which [Jesus] opened for us through the curtain, that is, through his flesh" (Hebrews 10:20). We can enter the holiest place—heaven—because we have been made "holy" by the blood of Jesus Christ (see Hebrews 10:19). We can enter confidently because God can make us saints, for only saints can enter God's presence and live (see Revelation 21:27).

Jesus' holiness must indeed have been communicable, for, upon his resurrection, "the tombs also were opened, and *many* bodies *of the saints* who had fallen asleep were raised" (Matthew 27:52). By the end of Jesus' earthly ministry, "many" people had been sanctified—had come to share somehow in God's holiness.

These are just hints here and there, of course, but they are evidence of a cosmic revolution. Holiness broke into the world when the Word became flesh, and it broke out in unexpected places. No longer in the reserve of Jerusalem's precincts, no longer exclusively amid the people of Israel, no longer confined to the twenty-four hours of the Sabbath, holiness had erupted into the ordinary lives of ordinary people everywhere.

THE "IN" CROWD

The idea of a shared holiness, hinted at in the Gospels, becomes a major theme in the letters of St. Paul, for the Apostle keeps no scruple about applying the word *saint* to human beings. He does so in the very salutation of his first letter that appears in the New Testament: "To all God's beloved in Rome, who are called to be saints" (Romans 1:7). Wow! Not only is he addressing fellow Christians as "holy" (*hagiois*), but he is saying that all the Christians in the Church of Rome have been "called" by God to that status.

Nor does he limit such holiness to the precincts of the imperial capital. He speaks, in the same letter, of "the saints at Jerusalem" (Romans 15:26). In his Corinthian correspondence he applies the term in a universal way—a *catholic* way—as he speaks of "all the churches of the saints" (1 Corinthians 14:33).

Nor is he addressing merely an elite group within each congregation. He addresses his Letter to the Philippians "To all the saints in Christ Jesus who are at Philippi, with the bishops and deacons" (Philippians 1:1), as if the clergy were an afterthought, a subset of the more important category: "the saints." And so they are.

Now, how did all those human beings—all those early Christians—suddenly come to achieve "holiness," a quality that had formerly belonged to God alone? We cannot chalk it up to a verbal slip on St. Paul's part. He does it too often, and he does it very deliberately. Remember: Paul was an esteemed scholar of the Hebrew Scriptures, and he certainly knew this most fundamental Jewish doctrine. He had been a Pharisee, a member of a sect that was dedicated to protecting God's holiness from defilement by the world. God's monopoly on holiness had been the foundation for Paul's understanding of the temple, the laws regarding purity, the special vocation of Israel, and everything else!

Yet there we see him, the greatest theologian of his age, using the term liberally and seemingly as a synonym for "Christian."

In fact, Paul never—not even once—uses the term *Christian* when he speaks of the members of the Church. He speaks instead of those who are "in Christ." And that's our key to understanding the sudden sanctity of human beings. If they are holy, if they are "saints," it is because they are "saints *in Christ*"—Christ who is holy, because he is God. (Think of Jesus as Midas, only his touch doesn't turn things into gold, he turns things holy.) The phrase *in Christ* abounds in St. Paul's letters, and it sums up his doctrine of Christian life.

Long before Jesus arrived, God had called Israel to be a "holy nation" (Exodus 19:6) when he freed the tribes from slavery in Egypt. But the Israelites forfeited that status almost immediately by their idolatrous worship of the golden calf (Exodus 32:1–6). So God gave them a detailed code of Law to serve as a remedy, a discipline, and a means of restoring their dignity. Still, they fell repeatedly into idolatry and immorality. On their own they could not live according to this Law, and so they could not live a righteous life, a life that was worthy of God's holiness. The Law, which was designed to be their help, helped them mostly by manifesting their ineradicable human weakness: their sinfulness. Through their inability to keep the law, their need for God became painfully apparent.

Merely human powers, and merely human nature, and merely human life were not enough to make anyone on earth lead a "holy" life. Even the Law could only take them so far. Only God could make someone holy. He wanted human beings to share in that life. And he *willed* that we should share that life. Yet we still missed the mark. We continued to sin. So what was God to do?

He didn't wait for us to achieve his life on our own power. He came instead to share our life. The Word became flesh in Jesus Christ. The eternal Son of God became the Son of Man so that the children of men might become the children of God. How can we do that? Again, the key is in St. Paul's preposition: We can share God's holiness because we are "in Christ." We have "become partakers of the divine nature," as St. Peter said (2 Peter 1:4). We share in God's divine nature because he has condescended to share in our human nature.

In the days of the Old Testament, the Jerusalem temple was the precinct of holiness. Now, however, Christ has declared that his body is the temple (John 2:21), and his body is the Church—and all the members of the Church are members of his body (see Acts 9:4–5 and Ephesians 2:19–22). They are "in" him, and he is "in" them.

"For you know the grace of our Lord Jesus Christ, that though he was rich, yet for your sake he became poor, so that by his poverty you might become rich" (2 Corinthians 8:9). We have become rich not in a worldly sense, but because God has given us all *his* riches: his life, a share in his nature, his holiness.

This is not a metaphor. It is the reality of salvation. Yes, we have been saved *from* our sins, and that is a marvelous thing; but, more importantly, we have been saved *for* sonship. As the Church Fathers put it, we have become "sons in the Son." Christ is the "firstborn" of God the Father (Hebrews 1:6), but "in him" the Church has become "the assembly of the firstborn" (Hebrews 12:23).

In Christ, "we are children of God, and if children, then heirs, heirs of God and fellow heirs with Christ"

(Romans 8:16–17). What he has by nature, his divine life, he has shared with us by grace.

If we can now achieve holiness, it is because we have become members of the divine household, the divine family (Ephesians 2:19). We have come to share *the life of the Blessed Trinity*. That life is the very definition of heaven, but it is given to us even now as a pledge.

"Receive the Holy Spirit," Jesus told his Apostles (John 20:22), *and then he gave them the Spirit!* The third Person of the Blessed Trinity came to dwell in their hearts. And now he has come to dwell in ours. "God's love has been poured into our hearts through the Holy Spirit which has been given to us" (Romans 5:5). That isn't just a warm, cuddly feeling. To receive the Holy Spirit is to receive sainthood. The Holy Spirit is the great saint maker. After all, "holy is his name." Saint is his name.

It is by the Spirit we are reborn as saints (Titus 3:5), and by the Spirit that we speak as saints (1 Corinthians 12:3), and in the Holy Spirit that we rejoice as saints (Romans 14:17). Our very bodies are temples of the Holy Spirit (1 Corinthians 6:19). The Spirit bears witness that we are God's children, that we share the divine nature—that we are saints (Romans 8:15–16).

We have become saints, as St. Paul might put it, "in" the only saint—in God, because we have come to share Christ's divinized humanity in the life of the Church, in the sacraments he has entrusted to the Church.

GROWTH BY GRACE

Paul speaks with incredible force about the importance of baptism. In just one short passage (Galatians 3:24–29), we get an avalanche of information about the effects of baptism: (1) it brings about our justification (v. 24); (2) it causes us to be freed from the futile discipline of the law (v. 25); (3) it establishes us as children of God (v. 26); (4) it clothes us with Christ (v. 27); (5) it causes those who were formerly divided to be one "in Christ" (v. 28); and (6) it makes both Jews and Gentiles to be Abraham's offspring (v. 29).

It makes us live *in Christ*, as God's own family. Living in Christ, we are taken up into the life of the Trinity, even now. Baptism makes us a truly holy nation. It makes us *saints*. What we could never become by strength, stamina, and a will of steel—which we lack anyway—we become by the grace of God.

In the Old Testament, the bond between God and his people was described as a "covenant" bond (in Hebrew, *b'rith*; in Greek, *diatheke*). In the New Testament, the language of covenant recedes and gives way to a new Greek word: *koinonia*—communion. We are so close to Christ that we are "in" him and he is "in" us. *Communion* is the only English word that begins to convey the reality of this mutual, loving indwelling.

We should not miss the importance of Paul's use of the

word *communion*. It marks a radical shift in his understanding, and indeed a revolution in the history of our salvation. Before the coming of Jesus Christ, Greek-speaking Jews would *never, ever* use the word *koinonia* to describe relations between God and any human beings. This is one way they guarded the doctrine of God's transcendence. Nor would Hebrew speakers use their equivalent, *chaburah*, for that purpose. These words had been applied only to "horizontal," earthly relations between close friends or family members.

Now, however, the world could know such communion—with God!—through the sacraments Christ had entrusted to the Church. This is true of all the sacraments, beginning with baptism (Matthew 28:19), but continuing most especially in the Eucharist and Confession (see 1 Corinthians 11:24, John 20:21–23), the two sacraments we may (and should) receive frequently. Paul describes the Eucharist as the means by which God's incarnation is extended through the Church by the power of the Spirit. He speaks in terms of communion in Christ's body and blood. "The cup of blessing which we bless, is it not a [*koinonia*] in the blood of Christ? The bread which we break, is it not a [*koinonia*] in the body of Christ?" (1 Corinthians 10:16).

These sacraments are the ordinary way that human beings may become holy—the ordinary way mere mortals may share in eternal life. To receive the sacraments is to live in Christ, to be members of his body, to dwell in his holy temple. It is to live in the Church through the life

Christ gave to his Church. It is to be a Christian. "Because there is one bread, we who are many are one body, for we all partake of the one bread" (1 Corinthians 11:17).

St. Ignatius of Antioch, a man of the first century who knew the Apostles, evoked all the terms of the Old Testament priesthood—temple, worship, and holy things—but showed them to be fulfilled in the New Testament, and not only in Christ, but in every Christian: "So you are all participants together in a shared worship, God-bearers and temple-bearers, Christ-bearers, bearers of holy things!"[2]

We are participants *together*. Thus, none of us lives merely alone with God. Together, as the Church, we bear God, bear Christ, bear the temple, and bear all holy things. Christ did not come to create a loose association of individuals, each of them living as "just me and Jesus."

In communion with Christ, you and I are members of his body, his Church, together with our fellow Christians. In communion we are saints. Granted, we don't have the monikers of those men and women who have been canonized, but we exist in holiness. Remember that the next time you get angry at a neighbor or stranger.

We are the assembly of the firstborn, we are Christians, we are the Catholic Church, we exist in *koinonia*, we are the holy ones, we are the *Communion of Saints*.

3

FOR *ALL* THE SAINTS

THERE ARE NO BARRIERS BETWEEN SAINTS. We have seen that "saints" are those who live in heaven, and "saints" are those who sit next to us in the pew on Sunday. These populations interrelate and interact, and they coexist in a special kind of community. We call it a "*Communion* of Saints," and it's worth our time to examine the scriptural foundations of the term.

A true Catholic could address any church with the terms St. Paul used in greeting the Corinthians, for every parish is the assembly of "those sanctified in Christ Jesus, called to be saints" (1 Corinthians 1:2). In baptism every Christian has been "sanctified," and God calls every Christian to persevere in holiness. Yet God calls no one to go it alone. We draw strength from one another, and we are, all at the same time, drawing strength from God. St. Paul emphasizes that we are "called to be saints *together* with all those who in every place call on the name of our Lord Jesus Christ" (1 Corinthians 1:2).

We live in a vast community with "all those" in "every place" who share our calling. This is as true of Christians in Colossae as it is of Christians in Corinth. St. Paul addresses the Colossians as "*saints* and faithful brethren in Christ" (Colossians 1:2)—and he notes that he has heard of the love they have "for *all the saints*" (1:4), meaning those who live not only in Colossae, but everywhere else on earth. And then the Apostle goes a step further. He goes on to give "thanks to the Father, who has qualified us to share in the inheritance of the saints in light" (Colossians 1:12).

"The saints in light"—what could Paul mean by this phrase? He could only mean the "holy ones" who had already died and who already knew God's glory in its fullness, the faithful Christians who already live "in light" divine and who "see [God] as he is" (see 1 John 3:2).

The Communion of Saints, then, is not simply an earthly phenomenon, not just a fancy title for the Sunday congregation and Wednesday Bible study. It is at once earthly and heavenly. As the Letter to the Colossians shows us, it is an "inheritance" we already "share" with those who are already enjoying it for all it's worth.

The New Testament consistently testifies to this bond between believers alive on earth and those who are more alive in heaven. We are mistaken, in a sense, when we refer to them as "the dead." Their bodies may have died, but their souls live in Christ; they are, in fact, more alive than we are, because nothing obstructs them from God. They are now "in light." "For now we see in a mirror dimly, but then face to face. Now I know in part; then I shall understand fully, even as I have been fully understood" (1 Corinthians 13:12).

Every Sunday, when we go to Mass, we profess that "we believe in the communion of saints . . . and life everlasting." Yet Blessed John Henry Newman observed, "Nothing is more difficult than to realize that . . . all the millions who live or have lived . . . Every one of those souls still lives."[1]

Though it is abundantly clear in Scripture, and though we swear it's our religion, we have a hard time really believing it. "*Nothing* is more difficult," said Cardinal Newman.

It can be helpful—and consoling and comforting—to review exactly what the New Testament tells us about those who have passed through this life.

FREE, BUT NOT CHEAP

By the Pauline measure we become a saint at baptism, but no one's a Saint (that is, a "saint in light") till death. In other words: it ain't over till it's over. And really, it's only just beginning.

God has loved us first, and he has made us for himself. He "desires" our love, and so he leaves us free, for true love cannot be coerced. It cannot be commanded. It must be freely given. From the beginning God created us with that radical freedom: to choose him, or to choose ourselves instead.

In choosing God, however, we must prefer him to everything: sensory pleasure, worldly success, and lesser loves. It's not that we must reject these good things outright, but we must order them to the highest good, which is God, if we are to live in communion with that highest good. We must prefer nothing earthly to divine love, glory, and holiness. So enjoy your car or your job or your family, but realize that God comes first.

Our spirits are often willing to make that choice for God, but our flesh is weak. We enjoy the things of the world, even though they are passing away, and we wish to enjoy them more constantly, more immediately, and at almost any cost. Inevitably, this presents us with a moral crisis, an ordeal, in which we must choose between God and our disordered attachment to some earthly thing. For some people, that thing will be job security; for others, it will be an unhealthy romantic relationship. For some, the temptation may be to buy physical health at the cost of immoral medical practices. Others will face the temptation to grow rich at the expense of the poor. The possibilities are as endless and delightful as the things of this world.

When we read the history of God's people, we see that the true heroes are those who faced such an ordeal and chose to suffer for love rather than sin for self. Abraham and Job come to mind. They clearly fit the profile of a saint. But so many others were tested and failed. Think about the great falls of Adam and Eve, David and Solomon, and even Moses. Think about the fallen angels, who first chose a hell of selfishness over an eternity of love.

All of us are called to share God's life, and we must face our ordeal and choose God freely. The ultimate test is our death; only then can we be truly called saints—completed saints, "saints in light." I'll say it again: it ain't over till it's over. Not even the pope has the authority to canonize a living human being, because until our death we remain free to choose: for God or against him.

We face the choice for Christ—the choice for holiness— and we face it with every moral decision that arises during our earthly life. St. Paul said, "For we must all appear before the judgment seat of Christ, so that each one may receive good or evil, *according to what he has done in the body*" (2 Corinthians 5:10). The Book of Revelation states the matter from heaven's perspective: "Blessed are the dead who die in the Lord henceforth. 'Blessed indeed,' says the Spirit, 'that they may rest from their labors, for *their deeds follow them!*'" (Revelation 14:13; see also Revelation 19:8).

Is our freedom really that radical? Are we free even to forfeit the sainthood we have received by grace? The Scriptures make clear that we can.

Note then the kindness and the severity of God: severity toward those who have fallen, but God's kindness to you, *provided you continue in his kindness; otherwise you too will be cut off.* (Romans 11:22, emphasis added)

For if we sin deliberately after receiving the knowledge of the truth, there no longer remains a sacrifice for sins, but a fearful prospect of judgment, and a fury of fire which will consume the adversaries. A man who has violated the law of Moses dies without mercy at the testimony of two or three witnesses. How much worse punishment do you think will be deserved by the man who has spurned the Son of God, and profaned the blood of the covenant by which he was sanctified, and outraged the Spirit of grace? (Hebrews 10:26–29)

For if, after they have escaped the defilements of the world through the knowledge of our Lord and Savior Jesus Christ, they are again entangled in them and overpowered, the last state has become worse for them than the first. (2 Peter 2:20)

Our earthly life is made up of deeds freely chosen, for good or for evil, and the deeds we choose will follow us to judgment. The deeds of a saint are proof of the faith of a saint (see James 2:14–25). We are known by our fruits (see Matthew 7:16–20).

HELL OF A CHOICE

The call to holiness is universal. God "desires all men to be saved and to come to the knowledge of the truth" (1 Timothy 2:4). While he created us free and respects that freedom, God does not wish "that any should perish, but that all should reach repentance" (2 Peter 3:9). He made everyone to find fulfillment by sharing the divine life. St. Augustine put the matter poetically: *You have made us for yourself, O Lord, and our hearts are restless until they rest in you.* Even so, we are free, and so we may prefer that restlessness to God, and we may make our permanent choice for a selfish restlessness.

Hell can be defined as the choice of self over God. Since this is a book about angels and saints and not about "last things" more generally, I'll save that particular discussion for a future book (God willing). Here I will simply acknowledge that the Scriptures speak clearly to us about the existence of hell and the very real possibility of our choosing it, in spite of the best preparation God, the Church, and our parents have given us. Again, hell is not so much a place of punishment as the guarantor of love. We cannot truly love God unless we can freely choose *not* to love him. Hell is the choice not to love God. It is the choice to prefer something else to God.

The New Testament speaks often of hell. In fact, Jesus and St. John—the historical figures best known for preaching about love—speak rather graphically about the fact of hell. Indeed, from the pages of Scripture we may know more details about hell than about heaven.

But it's heaven we came to *these* pages to discuss. So let's move onward and upward—heavenward.

REASONS FOR HOPE

St. Augustine, in one of his greatest works, examined the Communion of Saints according to a single metaphor: the *City of God*. Its citizenship, he said, includes souls already in heaven and folks on earth. Yet its earthly citizenship is not limited to those who are enrolled in a parish. St. Augustine held that many who did not profess Christianity were Christians unawares. Meanwhile, he said, some others who were card-carrying Christians were really living by the laws of another city, the City of Man. Yet in this world the two cities are mixed together, like the wheat and tares in Jesus' parable about the field, or the fish and trash in his parable about the net.

While we're on earth, we can't know which way another individual is tending. The agnostic who struggles may be clawing his way toward sanctity. The pew-warmer who never misses Sunday Mass may go home every week to indulge secret vices behind closed doors. Only God keeps the census rolls of the Communion of Saints. He sees what we do not.

And we never know how any individual story will end. True love is proved through the ordeal, the trial, the testing, the temptation; and sometimes the results are surprising. Listen to the Prophet Ezekiel:

> But if a wicked man turns away from all his sins which he has committed and keeps all my statutes and does what is lawful and right, he shall surely live; he shall not die. None of the transgressions which he has committed shall be remembered against him; for the righteousness which he has done he shall live. Have I any pleasure in the death of the wicked, says the Lord God, and not rather that he should turn from his way and live? But when a righteous man turns away from his righteousness and commits iniquity and does the same abominable things that the wicked man does, shall he live? None of the righteous deeds which he has done shall be remembered; for the treachery of which he is guilty and the sin he has committed, he shall die. (Ezekiel 18:21–24)

If a wicked man turns to God, he'll be ... a saint! If a seeming saint sails sinward—sad to say—he's chosen a hell of a future. God has called each of us to sainthood. So each of us has the God-given potential, and the God-given freedom, to choose our path whenever two roads diverge in our moral woods. We can go either way.

If there were social-networking software to track our dealings with God, the relationship status, for many people perhaps, would be stuck on "It's Complicated."

But they do get simpler. God has provided for that, and his provision should give us hope.

The Church has always taught that before passing to heaven, a soul undergoes some purification—to rid it of the relics of sins committed during earthly life, for "nothing unclean shall enter" heaven (Revelation 21:27). Jesus alluded to this intermediate state when he spoke of forgiveness after death (see Matthew 12:32) and when he spoke, metaphorically, of our sin as a debt we must repay (see Luke 12:58–59). St. Paul described it, again metaphorically, in terms of the building of a temple, where all the building materials must be purified like gold through fire (1 Corinthians 3:15).

Along the historical way, this process picked up the name *purgatory*, and the early Church Fathers (and Mothers) attest to it: Tertullian, St. Perpetua, St. Cyprian, Origen, St. Macrina and her brother St. Gregory, St. Augustine and his mother, Monica, and St. John Chrysostom, among others. C. S. Lewis, who was Protestant, believed in purgatory's existence, not merely on the basis of Scripture and tradition, but also, he argued, because purification—a chance to wash up—was a necessary mercy for anyone about to enter the throne room of the King of Kings.

Purified by God, we leave our complications behind and join the "saints in light."

4

WHAT DO SAINTS DO?

WHAT CAN IT MEAN FOR SAINTS ON EARTH to be "in communion" with saints who have died and gone to heaven or purgatory?

The life of the departed, at least for now, is purely spiritual. We, on the other hand, have a spiritual life, as they do, but we also have a bodily life that can dominate our consciousness.

We appear to be living very different sorts of lives, and this fact raises some practical questions about how "saints" relate to one another in God's great communion. After all, what could we possibly have in common with the saints in glory? What could be the basis of our friendship with them? And how do they affect our relationship with Jesus?

In St. Luke's Gospel (16:19–31), Jesus tells a story that sheds some light on our questions:

There was a rich man, who was clothed in purple and fine linen and who feasted sumptuously every day. And at his gate lay a poor man named Lazarus, full of sores, who desired to be fed with what fell from the rich man's table; moreover the dogs came and licked his sores. The poor man died and was carried by the angels to Abraham's bosom. The rich man also died and was buried; and in Hades, being in torment, he lifted up his eyes, and saw Abraham far off and Lazarus in his bosom. And he called out, "Father Abraham, have mercy upon me, and send Lazarus to dip the end of his finger in water and cool my tongue; for I am in anguish in this flame."

But Abraham said, "Son, remember that you in your lifetime received your good things, and Lazarus in like manner evil things; but now he is comforted here, and you are in anguish. And besides all this, between us and you a great chasm has been fixed, in order that those who would pass from here to you may not be able, and none may cross from there to us."

And he said, "Then I beg you, father, to send him to my father's house, for I have five brothers, so that he may warn them, lest they also come into this place of torment."

But Abraham said, "They have Moses and the prophets; let them hear them."

And he said, "No, father Abraham; but if some one goes to them from the dead, they will repent."

He said to him, "If they do not hear Moses and

the prophets, neither will they be convinced if some one should rise from the dead."

First of all, we should acknowledge that Jesus is telling a story here and not recording a historical event. Still, I believe the details of the story can teach us something about the afterlife. Jesus' narratives may have pointed to otherworldly things, but they always had the ring of worldly verisimilitude—the likeness to truth. They corresponded to reality, even when they were parables or "fictional."

Some commentators say that this story places the rich man in hell, but that seems unlikely, for many reasons. In the text, Jesus mentions the man's location as *Hades*, the abode of the dead, which Jews distinguished from *Gehenna*, the place of everlasting torment—the state we usually refer to as *hell*. What's more, the rich man is capable of communicating with the patriarch Abraham, something that would surely be impossible for someone in hell. And Abraham addresses him tenderly as "Son"!

Finally, and perhaps most tellingly, the man is still capable of charitable impulses. When he cannot satisfy his own desires, he begs help for his brothers who are still alive on earth. Such kindness would be impossible in hell, whose inhabitants have fallen entirely into the misery of self-absorption. Thus, we may conclude, as other commentators have, that the man is undergoing purification in purgatory.

But his cosmic GPS coordinates are not our primary

concern. What's interesting is that he and Abraham are clearly in the "afterlife," yet they are aware of one another and they are aware of life on earth. They remember their earthly days and their bonds of affection and kinship. What's more, they are capable of communicating with one another.

(Was the rich man refused in the end? It's interesting to note that, in real life, Jesus actually *did* raise a man named Lazarus from the dead and send him back to his people. See John 11:43–44. It's at least possible that this story is not simply a fictional parable. Indeed, if it were simply a parable, it would be exceptional. In no other parable does Jesus speak of a character by name. The name must somehow be significant.)

We glimpse in this story what the Church calls the "communication of spiritual goods." It is just a glimpse, but in the later books of the New Testament the situation becomes much clearer, as the heavens are thrown open to our view.

DRAWING A CROWD

What Jesus presents in miniature, the Letter to the Hebrews and the Book of Revelation depict on a grand and even colossal scale. Jesus brings out one patriarch, Abraham. The Letter to the Hebrews (chapter 11) evokes Abraham, too, but also Abel, Enoch, Noah, Isaac, Sarah, Jacob,

Joseph, Moses, Rahab, Gideon, Barak, Samson, Jephthah, David, Samuel, and the prophets. The author praises them, one and all, for their faithfulness.

Not to be outdone, the Book of Revelation speaks of a cast of hundreds of thousands, a multitude beyond counting.

And all of those saints are—right now—intensely aware of events on the planet earth. More than that, they are intensely *involved* in those events, and in communication with the "saints" still on earth: the Christians in the churches.

After listing off the names on that Old Testament all-star roster, the Letter to the Hebrews informs us that they're not just items on a memorial plaque. In fact, it says we are encircled by them: "we are surrounded by so great a cloud of witnesses" (Hebrews 12:1). They surround us now, and they are watching us, aware of us. Hebrews 12 depicts a liturgical assembly—a congregation at Mass—and that is where we know the presence of the saints in a powerful way, since the Mass is the act of worship that unites the hosts of heaven with the Church on earth. (More on that in a bit.)

When the Book of Revelation shows us the saints in heaven, they're engaged constantly in worship, and it bears all the marks of the Holy Mass: an altar, candles, vested priests, hymns like the "Holy, Holy, Holy" and the "Alleluia" and songs to the "Lamb of God." John testifies that he "saw under the altar the souls of those who had been slain for the word of God and for the witness they had borne; they cried out with a loud voice, 'O Sovereign Lord, holy and true, how long before you will judge and avenge our blood on those who dwell upon the earth?'" (Revelation 6:9–10).

Note that they are pleading with God for those who remain on earth. They have knowledge of God and knowledge of earthly happenings. They have concern, and they express their concerns, like children before a loving Father. They are asking God to intervene in history as it plays out after their own martyrdom.

Their prayers, not surprisingly, are answered. They are reassured that God will triumph, though persecutions will continue for a while. God will, however, vindicate them and the Church. "Then they were each given a white robe and told to rest a little longer, until the number of their fellow servants and their brethren should be complete, who were to be killed as they themselves had been" (Revelation 6:11). Knowing the future, these martyrs have greater knowledge than the saints on earth. They are sharing more fully in God's life and holiness. What we saw in the Letter to the Hebrews is borne out by the Apocalypse: God has blessed the martyrs for their faithfulness to his call—his call to share his holiness, to be saints.

The saints appear to be gathered in an assembly, a church, and engaging in ritual worship. Heavenly worship appears, however, in terms that are familiar from the sacraments of the Church on earth. "These are they who have come out of the great tribulation; they have washed their robes and made them white in the blood of the Lamb. Therefore are they before the throne of God, and serve him day and night within his temple" (Revelation 7:14). We see a little later (8:3) that the prayers of the saints are mingled with incense in a golden censer and placed upon a golden altar, "and the smoke of the incense rose with the prayers of the saints from the hand of the angel before God" (8:4).

What happens next is exhilarating. In response to the prayers of the saints, God calls upon the heavenly priests to blow their seven trumpets, evoking the Old Testament Battle of Jericho. As at Jericho, these trumpet blasts cause a tumult of earthly activity that vindicates the saints, avenges the blood of the martyrs, and takes down those who have been proud and haughty before God. All of this happens in response to the prayers of the saints. The point isn't argued in the Book of Revelation. It isn't debated. It isn't logically demonstrated. It's simply assumed and graphically described.

GOD'S CO-WORKERS, OUR INTERCESSORS

Jesus repeatedly commanded his saints to "love one another" (John 13:34, 15:12, and 15:17). The Apostles echoed that command (see Romans 12:10, 1 Peter 1:22, and 1 John 4:7). What is the best way for one saint to love another? St. James put it well: "pray for one another" (James 5:16).

Some people mistakenly believe that intercessory prayer—prayer that is offered by one saint for the sake of another—somehow undermines Jesus' status as our sole mediator. "For there is one God, and there is one mediator between God and men, the man Christ Jesus" (1 Timothy 2:5). Opponents of shared mediation often cite that passage from St. Paul's First Letter to Timothy. In order to do so, though, they must wrench it out of its original context, for it comes right on the heels of the Apostle's plea for the Church to intercede more assiduously!

"First of all, then, I urge that supplications, prayers, intercessions, and thanksgivings be made for all men, for kings and all who are in high positions, that we may lead a quiet and peaceable life, godly and respectful in every way. This is good, and it is acceptable in the sight of God our Savior, who desires all men to be saved and to come to the knowledge of the truth" (1 Timothy 2:1–2).

Jesus is not threatened when we imitate him by praying for our fellow saints. Nor is he offended. We may pray for one another (see, for example, 2 Corinthians 9:14). We should pray for one another. And we may ask others to pray for us (see, for example, 1 Thessalonians 5:25). And we should!

<u>We should ask prayers of all our fellow saints, those living</u>
<u>on earth and those who are more alive in heaven.</u>

Jesus is indeed the sole mediator between God and men, but he has willed that we should share his mediation, just as we share his life. It's all part of sharing the holiness of "the only saint." Jesus willed that we should co-redeem with him. Thus, St. Paul could say, "Now I rejoice in my sufferings for your sake, and in my flesh I complete what is lacking in Christ's afflictions for the sake of his body, that is, the Church" (Colossians 1:24).

Now, what could be lacking in the perfect suffering of Christ? Only what he willed to be lacking, for our sake—so that we could share his life, so that we could be his co-workers (1 Corinthians 3:9).

We believe in the Communion of Saints. <u>Communion is im-</u>
<u>possible without communication.</u> So we pray for one another. We ask prayers of one another. Nor must death shut us off in silence from the people we love—the *saints* we love. Through God's mercy, we may hope that many of our beloved are enrolled in that heavenly multitude.

We were made to live in the Communion of Saints. It's our nature to live in relationships. Without interpersonal relationships, a life is not fully human. God made us that way. The difficulty with friendship and kinship is that its earthly phase is finite. It's our sorrow that we must part from those we love. Yet it's our faith that relationships need not end.

Here's what the Church said through the Second Vatican Council: "Therefore the union of the wayfarers with the brethren who have gone to sleep in the peace of Christ is not in the least weakened or interrupted, but on the contrary, according to the perpetual faith of the Church, is strengthened by communication of spiritual goods."[1]

As our priests say during the Mass of Christian burial, "For God's faithful people, life is changed, not ended." This we know. Our hearts tell us so. The Church tells us so. The Bible tells us so.

5

TALKING ABOUT MY
VENERATION

S O WHAT SHOULD BE OUR ATTITUDE TOWARD
the saints? We should first of all be aware of them.
They are with us, cheering us on, as we saw in the
Letter to the Hebrews. We should be grateful to them for
their prayers, for, as we saw in the Book of Revelation,
their prayers are changing world history. We should be inspired to follow their example. We should be eager to impress them as they look on from the glory cloud, the great
cloud of witnesses.

Moreover, we should tell them so. We should thank
them for their prayers, ask them for their prayers, and call
them out as our witnesses.

We should keep their images—in icons or statues—as
reminders of what a human life can be and should be.

This is how we live in relationship with others. This
is how we live in a society. This is how we live in a family.
And the Communion of Saints is the perfect society. It is
the family as God created it to be. It is God's family.

In my home I do not hesitate to call upon my younger children to help me carry the groceries. I don't hesitate to ask the older kids to give me a ride to work. I keep photos of my children and grandchildren on the walls, and I smile when they catch my eye. Sometimes those photos serve as my reminders to phone, text-message, or e-mail the family members who now live in faraway cities.

I have photos, too, of my parents; the image of my father keeps his memory fresh for me, even twenty years after his passing. The image of my mom keeps her in my mind, and keeps the flame of my affection burning, even though she lives so far away.

When I do the same things for the saints—when I glance at their icons, when I ask them for help, when I express my affection for them—I am simply doing what comes naturally for a human being, but now I'm doing it for supernatural ends. Grace does not destroy nature, but rather builds upon it, completes it, perfects it, and elevates it.

There is nothing outlandish or even unusual about the way Catholics venerate the saints. I must admit, however, that when I was Protestant I used to think it was . . . well, unthinkable. I thought it was all "unscriptural" because I had learned a very different—and very selective—way of reading Scripture. But now, after a quarter century in the Church, I find it rather odd that some Christians *don't* honor the saints with devotion.

After all, why wouldn't we celebrate their feast days when we're eager to observe our own family's birthdays and anniversaries? Why should we mark Washington's birthday, but not the feast of Saints Peter and Paul?

Why should we raise statues of presidents and governors in our parks and town squares, yet forbid statues of the Blessed Virgin Mary?

Why raise colossal monuments to the founding fathers of our nation, yet refuse to name shrines in honor of the Fathers of the Church?

Why speak of military cemeteries (or any cemeteries) as "hallowed ground," as Abraham Lincoln did in his Gettysburg Address, yet disdain to give special honor to the relics of the saints?

Misguided people sometimes accuse Catholics of "idolatry" for keeping images of the saints. The charge is unjust and untrue. We do not give to images the honor that is due only to God. We don't *worship* icons of the saints any more than our neighbors worship photos of their grandchildren. Technically, we don't even venerate the icons, but rather the persons who are represented by the icons.

Even then, we do not venerate the saints themselves with the kind of worship that is due to God alone. It is God who created the saints. It is God who blessed them and elevated them for our imitation. To him we give the glory, and to him we render thanks. One of the early Church Fathers, St. John of Damascus, made the classic distinction between *latría*, which is the adoration we give to God, and *dulía*, the veneration we give to our parents, our country, the cross, the Bible, and the saints.

Veneration is simply honor, and it is *due* honor. We pay "respect to whom respect is due, honor to whom honor is due," as the Apostle exhorted us (Romans 13:7).

Furthermore, as we bless the saints, we are imitating Jesus Christ, for he has blessed them first. "Blessed are the dead who die in the Lord" (Revelation 14:13). "Blessed are those who are invited to the marriage supper of the Lamb" (Revelation 19:9).

Let's go back to the beginning, to the Book of Genesis, so that we can understand the nature of the covenant God has made with us. As he made his family bond with Abraham, God said, "I will bless those who bless you, and him who curses you I will curse; and by you all the families of the earth shall bless themselves" (Genesis 12:3). In the next generation, as Isaac blessed his son Jacob, he echoed God's words: "Let peoples serve you, and nations bow down to you ... blessed be every one who blesses you" (Genesis 27:29).

We bless God who is blessed over all, and then we bless those whom he blesses, because that is the nature of the covenant. When we bless the saints, when we honor them, we are blessed in turn.

We certainly don't pray to the saints *instead* of Christ. We pray *through* the saints *to* God *in* Christ. Ultimately, the saints don't answer our prayers. They echo our prayers with greater profundity, insight, and love. So say the Scriptures: "The prayer of a righteous man has great power in its effects" (James 5:16).

So why bother going to them and not directly to God? Because God made us to live in a family. He made us to live in society. He made us to live in communion—the Communion of Saints.

God made us to draw together with one another as we draw closer to him. He wants us to keep good company. When we stay close to the saints, we're keeping close to, and communicating spiritual goods with, the best of the best.

PATRONS AND BENEFACTORS

When the early Christians pondered this cosmic "economy," they compared it to earthly realities with which they were familiar. They considered it in light of the "patronage" system.

Patronage was one of the fundamental ordering principles of societies in ancient times. It was based on the idea that great wealth entailed great responsibility. Rich people were responsible for "patronizing" those who had less, providing them employment opportunities and so on. We can see it at work in the New Testament, in the requests people made of Jesus. Consider the request made by the ambitious mother of James and John: "Command that these two sons of mine may sit, one at your right hand and one at your left, in your kingdom" (Matthew 20:21). She wished her sons to be the highest-ranking "clients" of the world's most powerful patron. In the later New Testament books, we see that the Apostles did indeed come to occupy the position of "patrons" in the nascent Church, with disciples petitioning them for favors (for example, Acts 3:23).

The patronage system provided a convenient and *natural* illustration of the *supernatural* order of the communication of spiritual goods. The "saints in light" are now sharing in God's knowledge, power, and wisdom. They are more fortunate than the saints-in-training who continue to struggle here on earth. They are aware of our plight (as we saw in the New Testament books of Revelation and Hebrews). They are, moreover, participating in God's eternal charity, and so they seek our highest good.

Here, however, the patronage system was purified of its earthly abuses. And it was turned on its head. Rather than patrons choosing clients, as was the case in the earthly empires, in the communion of saints we find clients choosing patrons! From the early centuries of the Church, congregations *chose* the patron saint for whom their parish would be named. Individuals *chose* the saints to whom they would be especially devoted.

We see an important spiritual principle at work here. To be perfected, in a Christian sense, is to become more God-like. It is to become more like God the Father—more fatherly, more paternal. And that is the quality of a perfect patron. The very root of the word *patron* is *pater*, the Latin and Greek word for "father."

To be so godly is to share in God's perfect charity, and

then to share that love lavishly with others. That is what the saints do. That is why Christians have always sought their patronage.

In the early Church, we see the beginnings of a certain differentiation among the saints. By popular demand, certain saints were assigned certain patronal duties. Sometimes these were based on details of their earthly biographies. Sometimes their patronage was based on a miracle worked through their intercession in the afterlife. A parish in Rome, for example, might be named "San Lorenzo" because St. Lawrence lived or died there. On the other hand, an Egyptian Christian might go to St. Menas for healing not because Menas was a physician in life—in fact, he was a soldier—but because the miraculous spring at his shrine was known to have curative power.

Some of the earliest-named churches (that we know about, anyway) were named for St. Michael the Archangel, simply because he was the most powerful guardian against evil (see Revelation 12:7, Jude 9, and Daniel 12:1). And we're always in need of that kind of patronage.

GOOD TO THE BONE

Regard for the relics of the saints was a distinctive Christian practice at a very early date. We read in the earliest accounts of martyrdom that, by the mid-100s, Roman officials recognized this and sought to destroy and disperse the martyrs' bodies, so that the Christians were denied what was already perceived as a source of spiritual power. We find this in the contemporary accounts of the martyrdom of St. Polycarp (155 AD) in what is now the land of Turkey. The lack of earthly remains did not, however, diminish his spiritual influence or the ardor of Christian devotion to his memory.

The Book of Revelation (6:9) attributes such power to the souls of the martyrs, which are depicted as resting under heaven's altar. Perhaps based on this image from the Apocalypse, Christians took up the practice of building their altars over the tombs of the martyrs—or encasing the saints' remains inside the church's altar. Catholic parishes still do this today.

Such tender care for the saints' bodies was a hallmark of Christian life, and is evident in the documents of the early Church, from *The Passion of St. Perpetua* to the biblical commentaries of St. Jerome and the sermons of St. Augustine.

The veneration of relics set Christians apart from their contemporaries. Both pagans and Jews had a horror of corpses and believed that contact with a corpse rendered a person unclean and unfit for worship. Christians, however, believed that the bodies of the saints had come to share in the divinized humanity of Jesus, and so they shared in Jesus' divine power to forgive and heal. When St. Perpetua's jailer, Pudens, underwent a conversion of heart, he received from one of the dying martyrs a ring soaked in blood. It was a gesture that would have been repugnant to him as a pagan, only a few days before. Yet it is a gesture that came naturally and supernaturally to a second-century Christian.

This is what we do in Christian families, and in the great Christian family of the Church. We care for our dead and their remains. We house the relics of our saints in cemeteries, and then we call the ground "holy," for the bodies there have shared the body of Christ, who alone is holy.

As Christians, we've read the Book of Revelation and we live it, with Christ and with his saints. We know that the human race has a mortality rate of one hundred percent. Yet we also know that the human race has an immortality rate of one hundred percent. The idea has profound and far-reaching consequences.

6

A GATHERING OF ANGELS

WE'VE TAKEN A LONG LOOK AT THE Communion of Saints—the Church—the City of God—and found it to be much larger, perhaps, than we'd ever known. Yet we haven't uncovered even *half* of its citizenry, for we've considered only the human minority.

That's right: the human *minority*.

Since the earliest days of the Church, Christian preachers and commentators have reflected on the Scriptures and concluded two things: (1) the Church is the common dwelling of not only saints but angels as well, and (2) there are many more angels than there are people.

How do they crunch the numbers? They begin with Jesus' observation that everyone has a guardian angel (see Matthew 18:10). That, right away, would require an equal number of angelic and human beings. But then they add in the great number of other angelic beings who appear in the Bible—thousands upon thousands of cherubim, seraphim, thrones, dominions, principalities, hosts, and powers. Pretty soon, it starts to add up.

St. Augustine devotes a great portion of his *City of God* to the consideration of the city's majority. He defines the citizenship as including, simply, "the good, angels as well as men."[1]

The angels share in our great communion. They share in our worship. And they share in communication with us. This is apparent throughout the Bible, but especially in the New Testament.

St. Augustine points out that angels appear everywhere in the Scriptures. They make their debut in the Bible's opening line: "In the beginning God created the heavens and the earth." By "heavens" the author could not have intended the "skies," as the creation of the skies comes later in the narrative. St. Augustine also taught that God's command "Let there be light" (Genesis 1:3) was actually the decree by which he made the angels—before the sun and the other lights of the material world. Thus, God himself, from the very beginning, gives a certain primacy to the spiritual. When Genesis describes the separation of light from darkness (v. 4), it is recounting the rebellion of Satan and the demons (see Revelation 12:4) who chose everlasting darkness for themselves. This must have preceded the sin of Adam and Eve, because the primal couple gave in to demonic temptation (Genesis 3:1–6).

Since the time of the primordial fall, humanity has been beset by evil spiritual forces and defended by good spiritual forces. We call this struggle "spiritual warfare." In the Old Testament, the human race presented a weak defense against evil, and so even the good angels had to rule with a heavy hand, like babysitters entrusted with the care of unruly children (see Galatians 4:1–3). When angels appeared to human beings, the humans fell down in awe and profound fear, for angels are mighty beings (see Numbers 22:31, Tobit 12:16).

THE PLACE OF ANGELS

Like God, angels are pure spirits, immaterial. Like us, though, they are creatures, and they are finite. They had a beginning. Though they are mighty in power, their powers are limited.

Like us, the angels are free, and God gave them the choice to love him or not.

The glossary appended to the English edition of the *Catechism of the Catholic Church* defines *angel* concisely as "A spiritual, personal, and immortal creature, with intelligence and free will, who glorifies God without ceasing and who serves God as a messenger of his saving plan." That is a tidy summary of the biblical data.

We may note, however, that with the New Testament came an immediate change in the way the angels dwell within the Church. They no longer treat human beings as wayward children. Instead, they *serve* us. They guide us and guard us. They worship beside us. Sometimes they even appear, at their own insistence, to be our equals!

The primary example of this, of course, is the Angel Gabriel's deference toward the Virgin Mary in the scene of the Annunciation (Luke 1:28). He speaks to her not as a superior addresses a subject, but rather the opposite. He is speaking to his queen.

The first generation of Christians enjoyed the service of the angels and observed a remarkable degree of familiarity with them. Consider chapter 12 of the Acts of the Apostles. After an angel frees Peter from prison, he goes to the door of the house church. There, the congregation cannot believe it's really Peter—but they have no trouble concluding that they are seeing his angel (see Acts 12:13–15).

The angels themselves encourage this sense of equality. In Revelation, when John sees an angel, he falls on his face, as his ancestors had done in the Old Testament. But the angel tells him to get up: "You must not do that! I am a fellow servant with you and your brethren who hold the testimony of Jesus. Worship God" (Revelation 19:10).

In the Church—in the Communion of Saints—God's holy people worship side by side with his holy angels. In the Old Testament, earthly worship was carried out merely in imitation of heavenly worship. Now, in Jesus Christ, heaven and earth have been united in a great cosmic liturgy, with angels and saints worshiping together. Heaven and earth are full of the same glory cloud—which had pre-

viously been confined to the Holy of Holies in the Jerusalem Temple.

For us on earth, this takes place in the Holy Mass,
where we regularly remind ourselves that we stand among
"all the angels and saints . . . And so with all the choirs of
angels we sing: *Holy, Holy, Holy* . . ." The Mass is the combined worship of heaven and earth—the fulsome worship
of the Communion of Saints.

ORDERING ANGELS

The Greek word *angelos* (like the Hebrew word *malach*)
means "messenger," but we apply it more generally to any
created spirit. All created spirits are now subject to the
Church, as we are. St. Paul reminds the Corinthians that
"we are to judge angels" (1 Corinthians 6:3), and St. Peter
says that the Church possesses mysteries "into which angels long to look" (1 Peter 1:12).

So the Church—even on earth—exercises a certain authority over these mighty spirits. We call upon St. Michael
the Archangel to defend us against Satan—and he comes
to our assistance! In the rite of exorcism, a priest or bishop
drives demons away from the person they have come to
possess, oppress, or torment. This is yet another example
of the power of binding and loosening, bestowed by Christ
to the clergy. Bishops and priests exercise this power on

earth, but it extends by grace even to heaven (see Matthew 16:19, 18:18).

One of the ancient Fathers, whom we know today by the name St. Denis the Areopagite, explained that the hierarchy of angels in heaven reflects the hierarchy of the Church on earth. Hierarchy means "sacred order" or "sacred rule." And God established this order, top to bottom, for the sake of service. Those who are "highest" in rank—that is, those who have received the greatest spiritual gifts—must serve all those who are "lower" in rank and bring them to greater knowledge of God. That is why, in the earthly Church, the pope is called "servant of the servants of God." He must serve you and me, and so must the most sublime among the angels.

PART II

7

ST. MICHAEL AND
THE ANGELS

WITH THIS CHAPTER WE MOVE FROM OUR general beliefs about the "holy ones" to see how the Catholic doctrine of the saints is lived out by individual persons. So we begin, as God did, with angels.

And perhaps we have to remind ourselves that each angel is indeed an individual *person*. We saw in the last chapter, as we see in the Bible, that angels are *personal* beings. They are *persons*, and so they have *personalities*— distinct vocations from God as well as distinguishing traits and qualities. The great theologians have argued that each angel is not only a separate person, but a species unto himself, since species in the material realm are categorized by physical difference, which angels lack.

Scripture suggests to us that angels are the ordinary means by which God gets things done—the way he guides world history, as seen in the Old Testament Book of

Daniel and the New Testament Book of Revelation. The ancient rabbis and the Church Fathers believed that angels also maintained the physical laws of the universe. They kept the stars in their courses, and they swelled the rivers when the time was right. Scripture reveals that individual human beings have guardian angels, and so do nations (see Daniel 10:13, 10:20, and 12:1) and churches (see Revelation 2:1, 8, and 12, for example).

Scripture tells us the names of only three angels: Michael, Gabriel (Daniel 8:16 and Luke 1:19), and Raphael (Tobit 5:4). Michael appears in three different books of Scripture: Daniel (10:21), Jude (9), and Revelation (12:7). Tradition places him in other biblical books as well, though he is not mentioned by name. Jews and Christians have, from ancient times, identified St. Michael as the special guardian of God's people on earth. According to this tradition, it is he who assists the armies of Israel in the Old Testament (see, for example, Joshua 5:13–14).

Even in heaven, St. Michael is mighty among the angels. The Book of Revelation (12:7ff) depicts him as the commander of the heavenly host of angels as they battle Satan and the rebellious spirits. St. Augustine identifies this battle as the moment when God separated the light from darkness at the beginning of creation (Genesis 1:4). We know how the battle ends, and we know Michael is victorious (see Revelation 12:10). Still, the war will rage on until the final consummation of history. Scripture suggests to us that conflict between earthly states has an unseen dimension in the heavens. Our troubles and our struggles in this world are not simply anxieties over material discomforts. They're also—and primarily—spiritual struggles. Spiritual combat. Spiritual warfare.

From the earliest days of the Church, Christians have invoked Michael as patron, guardian, and leader as they faced difficulties and persecution. The Roman emperors—from Nero to Diocletian—may have been the earthly manifestation of their battle. The primary threat, however, was not to the *physical* well-being of believers, but to their souls. Would they be faithful through the ordeal? Could they endure the external threats and mockery as well as the internal stresses (fear, uncertainty, and the desire for human respect)?

Alone, they could not do it. They knew that. The emperors were too powerful. Yet the Christians had the example of Jesus before them. When tempted, he had prevailed *with the assistance of angels* (see Mark 1:13). In the Garden of Gethsemane, when he was in *agony*—the Greek word literally means "battle"—he was comforted and assisted by an angel (Luke 22:43).

Now, why would Jesus call upon the angels for help? He is God, and so he is all-powerful. As the second Person of the Trinity, he had created the angels and given them whatever powers they had. Angelic power is mighty, but it is still limited, whereas God's is not. Jesus didn't need the angels' help.

So why did he accept it? Perhaps he did this so that we

could learn how it's done. He did it to show us the way the world works, not only in its visible and material manifestations, but in its invisible and spiritual workings as well.

From Jesus himself we have learned to go to the angels, and so we go to our personal guardian angels and St. Michael, too. We should know their presence, as Saints Peter and Paul did in the Acts of the Apostles. And we should speak with them, as St. John did in the Book of Revelation, and as the prophets did in the Old Testament. We may do this silently, in our souls. We are spiritual beings as the angels are, and we can communicate with them through the ways of prayer.

As we become familiar with them, we will be more attuned to their promptings as we go about our everyday life. We can approach not only our own guardian angels, but those of our family members—spouse, children, grandchildren—asking their help in building up our relationships. We can make them our partners in a holy conspiracy as we try to draw friends and neighbors and co-workers into a deeper life of faith.

It was customary, through most of the twentieth century, to invoke St. Michael's help at the end of every Mass. Congregations prayed the prayer promoted by Pope Leo XIII at the end of the nineteenth century—a prayer he composed, reportedly, after an extraordinary and ominous vision of spiritual warfare as it would unfold in the coming years.

St. Michael the Archangel, defend us in battle. Be our protection against the wickedness and snares of the devil. May God rebuke him, we humbly pray, and do thou, O Prince of the Heavenly Host, by the power of God, cast into hell Satan and all evil spirits who prowl about the world seeking the ruin of souls. Amen.

In the visions reported in the Books of Daniel and Revelation, St. Michael appears as playing a special role in the execution of divine justice and mercy. Thus he is often invoked at the hour of death. For this reason, deathbed prayers often call upon him.

The Church celebrates the feast of St. Michael and All Angels on September 29 and the feast of the Guardian Angels on October 2. We have a lot to celebrate on those days.

By God's design, the angels are active in our life, from the time we are conceived to the moment of our earthly end. Our moments go better if we work with the angels, as the Scriptures show!

PONDER IN YOUR HEART

In a letter to his beloved sister, St. Ambrose of Milan, a fourth-century Father of the Church, explains the providence of God as shown in the guardianship of the angels. He holds up the stories of the Prophet Elisha (2 Kings 6) and the Apostle Peter (Acts 12) as exemplars of Christian faith and devotion to the angels.

Elisha was sought after by the king of Syria. An army was sent to take him. He was surrounded on every side. His servant began to fear, because he was a servant—that is, his mind was not free, nor had he freedom of action.

The holy prophet prayed that his eyes might be opened, and said, Look and see how many more are on our side than against us. And he looked up and saw thousands of angels!

You see then that the servants of Christ are protected rather by invisible than by visible beings. But when they keep guard around you, they have been called to do so by your prayers; for you have read that those very men who sought for Elisha on entering Samaria came upon the very man whom they wished to capture, yet they were not able to injure him, but were saved by the intercession of the very man against whom they came.

Take the Apostle Peter, too, as an example of both these things. When Herod sought after and took him, he was put in prison; for the servant of God had not fled but stood firm and without fear. The Church prayed for him, but the Apostle was asleep in the prison, a proof that he feared not. An angel was sent to rouse him from his sleep, and by him Peter was brought out of prison and for the time escaped death.[1]

—ST. AMBROSE OF MILAN, *Letter 22.11*

8

HOLY MOSES

W E TEND TO THINK OF MOSES AS A MAN
of action. Our imagination has been formed
by movies like *The Ten Commandments*, which
portrayed him as an agglomeration of heroes from American history and legend. In the movie he is a military commander who overthrows tyranny, a liberator who frees
the slaves, a wonder-worker who pulls off amazing special
effects—some long-ago mash-up of George Washington,
George Patton, and Paul Bunyan, with Abraham Lincoln
thrown in for good measure.

And there's some truth to all that. The Exodus of Israel
from Egypt is indeed an action story, though its drama advances through human bungling more than heroism.

Still, Moses' place in world history and his accomplishments make other heroes' biographies look puny by comparison. His résumé was impressive; yet he was much more
than the sum total of his résumé.

He freed an entire nation from slavery. He faced

a disciplined military bent on destroying him and his people—and he prevailed, witnessing his opponents' utter defeat and destruction.

He restored his people's sense of national identity. He guided them over desert—and through the midst of the sea—to the land that would be their own. He established a law that, in turn, shored up the healthiest culture on earth. He traditionally gets the credit for composing the Torah, the Book of the Law, the first five books of the best-selling and most influential book of all time: the Bible.

We look at him. We read his story. And we see a man who should rightly be the envy of every king and president, general and lawmaker, author and artist, pundit and real estate mogul.

Yet none of those worldly achievements corresponds to the quality that the ancients—both Christians and Jews—found most important.

From antiquity we possess, apart from the biblical accounts, biographies of Moses composed by two men of genius: Philo of Alexandria, a first-century Jew, and St. Gregory of Nyssa, a fourth-century Christian. What's most interesting about these works is what they have in common: both treat Moses not so much as a man of action, though they recognize all his mighty deeds, but rather as a man of *contemplation*. Moses is, for Philo and for Gregory, the very model of a man of profound prayer. His life shows us how to live ours in the presence of God.

There are differences in emphasis between their studies. Philo emphasizes Moses' moral virtue. Gregory concentrates on Moses' prayer and spirituality and sees his life as a paradigm of our own as we pass through successive stages of purification, illumination, and union with God.

According to Scripture, Moses' distinguishing characteristic was his conversation with God. "Thus the Lord used to speak to Moses face to face, as a man speaks to his friend" (Exodus 33:11). His spirituality was the quality that defined his life and set him apart from those who came before him as well as those who came after him, throughout the period of the Old Testament. "And there has not arisen a prophet since in Israel like Moses, whom the Lord knew face to face" (Deuteronomy 34:10).

The author of the Book of Sirach treats Moses in his catalog of "famous men" from the past, and he dwells exclusively on Moses' spiritual gifts, his intimacy with God, his equality with the angels (see Sirach 45:1–5).

The early rabbis shared this emphasis. In the third century, the great Babylonian teachers Rab and Samuel agreed: "Fifty gates of understanding were created in the world, and all but one were given to Moses, for it is said, 'For thou hast made him [Moses] a little lower than God.'"[1] Elsewhere in the Talmud, we find Raba (fourth century) extolling Moses' superiority to every other seer and inspired author: "All the prophets looked into a dim glass, but Moses looked through a clear glass."[2] On another occasion, Rabbi Samuel went so far as to say: "The world was created for the sake of Moses, so that he might receive the Torah."[3]

What set Moses apart was his ability to set himself apart—to reserve a generous portion of time and space for familiar, intimate prayer. To do so is to begin a life like God's. It is to begin to imitate the "holiness" of God; the Hebrew word for holiness means, quite literally, "set apart."

How did this happen? Well, by God's design, of course, but also by Moses' free choice. When as a younger man Moses fled Egypt alone, he sought refuge in Midian and placed himself under the tutelage of a priest named Jethro (Exodus 2:21). He became a disciple. He looked for a spiritual director.

Moses worked at tending Jethro's flocks, but in the midst of his work he went to "Horeb, the mountain of God" (Exodus 3:1). He went to the place of God's presence, and there indeed he had his decisive encounter—not with Pharaoh, but with the Almighty—in the bush that was burning, yet not consumed. Moses was instructed to take off his shoes, "for the place on which you are standing is holy ground" (Exodus 3:5). The Lord God went on to reveal his name to Moses and issue a personal call, a vocation. Moses listened, and the idea seemed outlandish to him: that a nobody from nowhere should go all alone into the heart of Egypt's great cities, rousing the enslaved people, and confronting Pharaoh with his injustices. It sounds outlandish. But God can do *anything*, and Moses could do God's work because he had spent time apart with God in sustained and disciplined prayer.

Listen to the Church Fathers. Listen to the rabbis. It was Moses' special intimacy with God that made it possible for him to compose the Torah. He could describe the earliest days of creation not because he was there, but because *God was*; through prayerful intimacy, Moses had come to see as God saw.

It's not that Moses was perfect. He had serious defects and failings. In fact, he sometimes sinned grievously. He once murdered a man in the heat of anger (Exodus 2:12). He struggled with doubt, and he gave in to doubt (see Numbers 20:12).

But he always turned again to God, and he returned not only to "saying prayers," but living a life of prayer, and leading others to prayer—as many people as he could. He became a *mediator* for others, pleading the case of sinners and bargaining for their lives. He even offered his own life as a ransom for theirs, thus prefiguring the redemption that would be perfectly fulfilled in Jesus.

Moses himself promised that a prophet like him would one day arise (see Deuteronomy 18:15). God's saving words and deeds in Moses' lifetime would form a kind of template for what he himself would say and do to save Israel— and all the nations—in the faraway future.

Israel had passed through the waters of the Red Sea as God's beloved son; so Jesus would pass through water in baptism and be called God's Son. (Compare Matthew 3:17 with Exodus 4:22.) As Israel had left the waters to be tested in the desert for forty years, so Jesus would be driven from the baptismal waters to be tested in the desert for forty days. And each time Jesus rebuked his tempter, he quoted Moses!

As Moses had climbed a mountain to bring God's Law and covenant, so Jesus would climb a "mount" and deliver a new Law and a New Covenant. Moses commanded the Israelites to commemorate God's covenant in the Passover celebration (see Exodus 12). Jesus instituted a new Passover, the Holy Eucharist. As Moses had sealed the Old Covenant with the blood of sacrificial animals, Jesus would seal the New Covenant with his own blood. He even quoted Moses' words: "This is the blood of my covenant." (Compare Matthew 26:28 and Exodus 24:8.)

Jesus led a new Exodus: this time, not from a political tyrant whose armies are drowned in the sea, but from sin and death, which are destroyed in the waters of baptism.

Moreover, Jesus extended to all his disciples the gifts that formerly had been given only to Moses. Though "now we see in a mirror dimly," as the lesser prophets did, in heaven we will see God "face to face," as Moses did (see 1 Corinthians 13:12).

We may look at Moses in the movies and find him fascinating—yet irrelevant to our own spiritual lives. But that's not the Moses we'll meet in the pages of Scripture, as the Fathers and rabbis and Jesus did.

✣ ✣ ✣

The Moses we meet in Scripture is a *saint*, whose life invites imitation. Like Moses, you and I have a calling from God. Like Moses, we need time alone with God in order to discern it.

Like Moses, you and I must remain faithful through trials, in spite of our weaknesses. When we fail through sin, we must turn again to God, as Moses did.

Like Moses, we must do all we can to draw others to God, without discrimination, loving the entire "nation." Like Moses, we must be intercessors for our neighbors.

All the great things Moses accomplished, God accomplished in him. Those wonders were possible because of Moses' union with God, a foreshadowing that would be fulfilled in the union of Jesus' human and divine natures—and in our own sacramental communion.

Many Catholics today are surprised to learn that Christian tradition venerates Moses as a saint. Indeed he was invoked along with the Prophet Elijah in the long litany chanted at the beginning of the conclave that elected Pope Francis in 2013. Moses has been so honored since the earliest days, and ancient calendars mark his feast on September 4. Nor is Moses the only Old Testament figure so honored. There are feasts for Abraham, David, Elijah, and others.

When was he canonized? Well, it's arguable at least that Jesus himself confirmed Moses' sainthood and that his "canonization" took place on Mount Tabor at the Transfiguration (see Luke 9:30–31). There we find Moses very much alive, along with the Prophet Elijah, conversing with Jesus about the new exodus.

Even in death, Moses became an object lesson about the power of God's saints. In the New Testament Letter of St. Jude we read that the Archangel Michael had to shoo Satan away from Moses' body—from his relics. The scene would replay itself repeatedly around the bodies of the martyrs in every generation, with Christians taking the part of St. Michael. If the bones of the Prophet Elisha were so powerful that they could raise the dead (see 2 Kings 13:21), imagine what the relics of Moses could accomplish.

By his leadership, Moses led the tribes of Israel into the earthly promised land. By his prayer, he mapped out a path that all peoples, and all generations, might follow to heaven. He was a contemplative even as he lived a busy life in the middle of the world. We can be, too.

PONDER IN YOUR HEART

St. Cyril of Jerusalem spoke to his fourth-century catechumens about the prayer of Moses. Because Moses asked the Lord, St. Cyril says, he was given a glimpse of the Christ who was to come.

Moses says to [the Lord], "Show me your glory" (Exodus 33:18). You see that the prophets in those times saw the Christ, that is, as much as each was able. "Show me your glory ... that I may see you with understanding." But [God] says, "you cannot see my face; for man shall not see me and live" (Exodus 33:20).

For this reason, because no man could see the face of the Godhead and live, he took upon himself the face of human nature, that we might see this and live. And yet when he wished to show *even that* with a little majesty, when his face did shine as the sun (Matthew 17:2), the disciples fell down afraid. His bodily face—shining with less than the full power of him who made it, but according to the capacity of the disciples—still frightened them, so that they could not bear it. How, then, could any man gaze upon the majesty of the Godhead?

The Lord says: "You want a great thing, O Moses, and I approve your insatiable desire, and I will do this thing for you, but measured to your ability. I will put you in a cleft of the rock. Since you are little, you shall lodge in a little space" (see Exodus 33:22).[4]

—ST. CYRIL OF JERUSALEM,
   Catechetical Lectures 10.7

9

ST. PAUL, SON OF GOD

IT'S IMPOSSIBLE TO IMAGINE WHAT THE LAST two thousand years would have been like if St. Paul had not lived at the far end of them. All the years since then have borne the mark of Christianity—the sign of the cross—and so much of what we understand about Christianity, and especially about the cross, we have learned from the great Apostle to the Gentiles.

St. Paul was among the first Christians to set pen to paper to proclaim the Gospel. He looked upon the news of the day, as it unfolded, and interpreted it in light of God's previous marvels. He took the great heritage of Israel and renewed and retooled its language for his exposition of the New Covenant. St. Paul gave the Church the vocabulary it would use, ever afterward, to understand the life, death, and resurrection of Jesus.

We have St. Paul to thank for so much of what we call the Church. It's not that he was the "founder" of Christianity, as some people claim. But he did play a unique role in the early proclamation of the Gospel.

His name from birth was Saul, and he had been a Pharisee—an intensely devout and intelligent man. Saul studied in Jerusalem under Rabbi Gamaliel the Great, the most renowned scholar of his time. A normal part of that education would be to ponder deeply the books of the prophets and commit entire books of the Law to memory. So Saul knew the promises God had made to the chosen people, and he knew that God would be faithful. Like many Jews of the first century, he waited with longing for the promised Messiah, God's anointed deliverer. The Messiah would deliver Israel from its bondage and oppression and bring salvation from God. Some Jews of Saul's time believed that if all of Israel could keep the Law of Moses *for just a single day*, the Messiah would come immediately.

Saul worked zealously to hasten this fulfillment. He went so far as to *enforce* the strictest fidelity to the Law, hoping to bring about the Day of the Lord. It was for this reason that he persecuted the Christians (see Philippians 3:5–6). He thought they were abandoning the God of their ancestors in order to worship a man.

Then Saul learned that the day had already arrived. The Messiah was Jesus. And deliverance had come in a way no one expected.

In fact, several lifetimes of study could not have prepared Saul—or anyone else—for the astonishing climax of God's plan. Though the prophets had evoked images of a suffering Messiah, the national tradition had dwelt instead on the more abundant images of a conquering king who would expel the pagan rulers and reestablish true worship in the promised land. Such is the imagery we find in the Dead Sea Scrolls and other documents from the first century.

God had indeed fulfilled the expectations of Saul—and of Israel—but he did it in his own way. God fulfilled every expectation and then surpassed them all immeasurably.

Saul expected the Messiah to be a king who would restore the house of David. God sent his own eternal Son instead, incarnate as a Son of David.

Saul expected deliverance to bring peace, prosperity, and freedom to obey the Law of Moses. But God's idea of salvation was far greater: he would deliver his people from sin; even more than that, he would deliver them from death; and greatest of all, he would deliver them to share his own life. Salvation was not merely *from* something; it was *for* something. God delivered his people from sin so that they might become his sons and daughters.

Saul of Tarsus became St. Paul the Apostle, and we should not be surprised to learn that he spent much of his time pondering and preaching about God's greatest surprises.

When Paul spoke of deliverance, it was almost as if human language was inadequate to express what Jesus Christ had accomplished. He exhausted one metaphor after another. He used the terminology of the courtroom, saying that we have been justified—that is, acquitted in a court of law (see Romans 5:16–17). He drew analogies from the marketplace, to make the point that we have been "redeemed": "You were bought at a great price" (1 Corinthians 7:23; see also Titus 2:13–14). He drew military analogies, portraying us all as the object of a divine rescue mission (2 Timothy 4:18). He said we were "set free" from "slavery" (Galatians 5:1).

But all the metaphors seem to lead to one that is his favorite: our adoption as children of God. It would have been a grand thing if God had just delivered Israel from oppression. It would have been greater still if he had forgiven all the sins of a fallen world. But God did so much more in Jesus Christ. He brought about "redemption" for the sake of "adoption" (Romans 8:23)—"to redeem those who were under the law, so that we might receive adoption as sons" (Galatians 4:5).

Our adoption as God's children is the deepest meaning of salvation. It encompasses redemption, justification, sanctification, and all the others. "But when the goodness and loving kindness of God our Savior appeared, he saved us, not because of deeds done by us in righteousness, but in virtue of his own mercy, by the washing of regeneration and renewal in the Holy Spirit, which he poured out upon us richly through Jesus Christ our Savior, so that we might be justified by his grace and become heirs in hope of eternal life" (Titus 3:4–7).

Some non-Catholic interpreters would have us stop short of this reality. They put the focus instead on justification—and they interpret "justice" by the standards of the modern courtroom. But in doing so they are ignoring the cultural and religious context of St. Paul's many metaphors. Supremely important for him (as for all first-century Jews) was the idea of *covenant*. It was the covenant with God that constituted Israel as God's chosen people. Covenant created a family bond; with Jesus' New Covenant (1 Corinthians 11:25) that family bond was made immeasurably stronger. Salvation has made us like Jesus—children of God in the eternal Son of God (see Galatians 3:26); "partakers of the divine nature" (2 Peter 1:4). Fidelity to this covenant is what Paul intends when he uses terms like *justice* and *justification*.

St. Paul knew that God was not content to be merely our judge. He wished to be our Father (see Ephesians 1:5). And that—God's fatherhood and our adoption—is the very essence of salvation in Jesus Christ.

"It is the children of God who are led by the Spirit of God. You have not received a spirit that makes you fear returning to your former slavery; you have received the spirit of adopted sons that cries out *Abba, Father!* For it is the Spirit Himself who gives testimony along with our spirit that we are children of God. And if children, also heirs: Together with Christ, God is our inheritance" (Romans 8:14–17).

Paul traveled the known world to proclaim this Good

News, and to announce a Church that was not just a reservation for the righteous, but was rather universal, intended for a restored Israel together with the Gentile nations.

Of all the Apostles, it was Paul who most consistently kept the Church from receding back to the safety of a provincial reservation. It was Paul who kept the universal, Catholic vision. It was Paul who proclaimed the power of the sacraments of the New Covenant. In the end, it was Paul who was impelled by grace, together with Peter, to consecrate the city of Rome with his own blood, shed in martyrdom.

Even today, after so many centuries, Paul's letters convey a personality that's overwhelming, a drive that's urgent. It's as if he can't get the words out fast enough. We catch his excitement, but we can also be frustrated. He rarely takes the time to spell things out, and he assumes that we already know a lot about the Bible and about the times he lived in. But we shouldn't feel *too* bad when we find St. Paul difficult. Even St. Peter confessed that he found St. Paul's letters "hard to understand" (2 Peter 3:15).

When we read them, we sometimes feel as if we're being propelled forward by a hurricane, a tidal wave, or some other force of nature. But it's even stronger than that, because it's a force of grace. Look at those maps of the Apostle's missionary journeys. Ponder those wide swaths that run the length and breadth of an empire. Imagine the momentum that made such progress possible.

And then remind yourself that the same momentum

has not diminished. God's arm has not been shortened. When you read St. Paul, when you hear his words proclaimed in the liturgy, you're exposing yourself to the same force. And that can only be life-changing.

PONDER IN YOUR HEART

St. John Chrysostom, in the early fifth century, preached line by line through St. Paul's Letter to the Ephesians. He didn't get through the first lines, the salutation, without reminding his hearers that they were children of God and so called to be saints!

"To the saints who are also faithful in Christ Jesus: Grace to you and peace from God our Father and the Lord Jesus Christ" (Ephesians 1:1–2).

Notice that he calls them "saints." From the end of the letter, it is plain that he is applying the name to married people, children, and household servants. There he says: "Wives, be subject to your husbands" (Ephesians 5:22) and "Children, obey your parents" (Ephesians 6:1) and, "Slaves, be obedient to those who are your earthly masters" (Ephesians 6:5).

Think how great is our laziness right now, how rare is anything like virtue now, and how many virtuous men must have lived back then, when secular men could be called "saints" and "faithful."

"Grace to you and peace from God our Father

and the Lord Jesus Christ." Grace is his word; and he calls God "Father," since this name is a sure token of that gift of grace. And how so? Hear what he says elsewhere: "And because you are sons, God has sent the Spirit of his Son into our hearts, crying, 'Abba! Father!'" (Galatians 4:6).[1]

—ST. JOHN CHRYSOSTOM,
Homilies on Ephesians 1.1

10

ST. IGNATIUS OF ANTIOCH, GOD'S WHEAT

IN THE LETTERS OF ST. IGNATIUS OF ANTIOCH, we encounter one of the most startling and stunning voices of the generation that overlaps with the ministry of the Apostles. We possess seven substantial letters from his hand. They are the works of a man passionate for Jesus Christ, passionate for the Church, a man on a journey and on a mission—and yet the man himself eludes us, for he was a prodigy of self-effacement.

St. Ignatius wrote his letters as he made the journey by land and sea from Antioch in Roman Syria (Antakaya in modern Turkey) to Rome in Italy. He was traveling under military escort. He was on his way to the imperial capital to be executed for the crime of professing the Christian faith.

St. Ignatius was bishop of the Church in Antioch, a major military and commercial center and the "second city" of the empire. It was in Antioch that the disciples were first called Christians. The Apostles Peter and Paul had worked there to evangelize the city, and tradition names Peter as its first bishop. Ignatius usually appears in the lists as Peter's second successor.

He was likely a hearer of the Apostles, but we don't know. Some of the ancients say that he, as a child, received a blessing from Jesus himself. But, again, we don't know.

For all his passion for the apostolic faith, St. Ignatius never name-drops and never invokes his spiritual pedigree. He never mentions a detail of his discipleship, conversion, election, or ordination. In fact, he recounts no personal memories whatsoever. He offers no backstory. We don't know how he came to make his long journey to martyrdom. He never mentions a betrayal, denunciation, or trial. He assigns no blame and seems to hold no grudges.

We ache to know more about such a Christian. Yet it was his humility that made the letters so valuable as historical documents; he was completely absorbed not with himself or his own thoughts, but rather with the lives and preoccupations of his intended readers. His letters are literary masterpieces; more importantly, they are acts of selfless love.

Because of Ignatius's great love, he has left us an abundant record of the cares, concerns, and commonplace joys of the Church of his generation. They are pastoral letters, marked by their warmth and their encouraging tone. Ignatius was not working out a systematic theology. He was not offering an apologetic argument. He simply assumed that the faith was the same in every city he visited between Antioch and Rome, as diverse as those cities might be.

By the year 107, when Ignatius probably set down his letters, the faith was already well established, and what can we say about that faith?

It is Christ-centered—and it is clear about who and what Christ is. He is both human and divine, "God become man ... sprung both from Mary and from God."[1] In his letter to Polycarp, Ignatius points to a Savior "who is above all time, eternal and invisible, yet who became visible for our sakes; impalpable and impassible, yet who became passible on our account; and who in every kind of way suffered for our sakes."[2]

It is biblical. Ignatius is traveling under arrest, under military escort, so we may assume that he does not have a library at hand. Yet he alludes often to the Scriptures of both the Old and New Testaments. He assumes their unity and their common authority in the Church. "Jesus Christ is our only teacher. Of him even the prophets were disciples in the Spirit and to him they looked forward as their teacher."[3]

It is Catholic. Ignatius gives us our earliest witness to the use of the word *Catholic* (in Greek, *katholike*) to describe the Church of Jesus Christ. Today, creative scholars like to imagine earliest Christianity as a riot of communities gathered around rival teachers who barely had anything in common. Thus the "Johannine Church" congregated around John, while the "Pauline Churches" (a supposedly vastly different species) agglomerated around Paul, the "Petrine" around Peter, and so on. Yet there is not a shred of evidence for it. Ignatius alludes evenly to the New Testament works of both John and Paul, and he refers to Peter and Paul together as if they were brothers. He assumes that wherever he goes, the Church is The Church. Or as he himself put it, "wherever Jesus Christ is, there is the Catholic Church."[4]

It is Eucharistic. For Ignatius, the Church is gathered around the Eucharist, and the Eucharist is the principle of unity in the Church. Thus he exhorted the Philadelphians: "Take heed, then, to have but one Eucharist. For there is one flesh of our Lord Jesus Christ, and one cup to [show forth] the unity of his blood."[5] Note that he uses the word "flesh" (in Greek, *sarx*), which is a graphic term that could also be applied to the meat sold in the marketplace. He is not afraid to shock people with the Real Presence, as Jesus did in the "Bread of Life" discourse (John 6). Ignatius says that it is the very mark of heresy to deny the Real Presence: "They abstain from the Eucharist and from prayer, because they do not confess the Eucharist to be the flesh of our Savior Jesus Christ, which suffered for our sins, and which the Father, in his goodness, raised up again. Those, therefore, who speak against this gift of God, incur death in the midst of their disputes."[6]

It is sacrificial. Ignatius consistently applies the vocabulary of the ancient temple to the Christian liturgy. He speaks of the Eucharist as a sacrifice and the Church as an altar. The Church is also "the place of sacrifice." To be in communion with the Church was, for him, to be "within the altar"—a beautiful phrase, evocative of Revelation 6:9.

It is hierarchical. Everywhere he goes, Ignatius assumes he will find the laity served by three orders of clergy: bishop, priest, and deacon. "Your bishop presides in the place of God, and your presbyters in the place of the assembly of the Apostles, along with your deacons, who are most dear to me."[7] He told the Ephesians that the priests should be attuned to their bishop as strings are to a lyre. He told the Philadelphians that the hierarchy's unity was an earthly manifestation of the unity of the persons of the Godhead.

Its earthly center is Rome. Though Ignatius presided over the Church where the disciples were first called Christians—and though he was himself a successor to St. Peter as bishop of that city—he deferred to the *Church of Rome.* In every other letter he speaks as a teacher to his disciples, a father to his children. Only when he addresses the Church of Rome does he speak with a tone of deference, as a disciple to his teacher, a child to his parent. He addresses the Roman congregation in lavish terms as "the Church which is beloved and enlightened by the will of him who wills all things which are according to the love of Jesus Christ our God, which also presides in the place of the region of the Romans, worthy of God, worthy of honor, worthy of the highest happiness, worthy of praise, worthy of obtaining her every desire, worthy of being deemed holy, and which presides over love, is named from Christ, and from the Father, which I also salute in the name of Jesus Christ, the Son of the Father: to those who are united, both according to the flesh and spirit, to every one of His commandments."[8] He reserves such superlatives for the Church that "presides over love" (*agape*, "charity") in the world. This is the earliest testimony to Roman primacy we have from a non-Roman author.

Ignatius's letters are also an inadvertent witness to the honor the early Church gave to those who suffered for the faith. Ignatius became a visiting celebrity in all the eastern churches, simply because he was on his way to martyrdom. His condemnation conferred upon him a sort of universal authority. Christians everywhere recognized him as a living saint. Ignatius, for his part, reveres others who have traveled the same route to martyrdom; he mentions them by name in his letters. Martyrdom (even anticipated martyrdom) was an imitation of Christ, a proof of sanctity. Indeed, Ignatius's letters would not have survived if people did not remember him with reverence. Just a few years after his passing, one of his correspondents, St. Polycarp of Smyrna, invoked the memory of Ignatius in his own letter to the Philippians (which has also survived).

Ignatius lived and died as if to illustrate his own theological principles. He preached a God who had given himself entirely in the Incarnation; who had given himself entirely in his passion and death; who had given himself entirely in the Eucharist. Ignatius, a priest of that God, identified himself with a love that is divine and self-giving. As he approached his final ordeal, he imagined his martyrdom as a sacrifice. He imagined it in Eucharistic terms. Surely he reminded himself often of Jesus' words: "Truly, truly, I say to you, unless a grain of wheat falls into the earth and dies, it remains alone; but if it dies, it bears much fruit" (John 12:24).

In his life, in his letters, and in his death Ignatius left us a vivid and permanent record of what it meant to be a Christian in the first and second centuries—and a prescient reminder of what it should mean in the twenty-first.

PONDER IN YOUR HEART

St. Ignatius prepared for his death as if he were preparing to celebrate Mass. He urges the Romans not to do anything to prevent his martyrdom. He imagines them attending his death as a liturgy.

If you are silent concerning me, I shall become God's; but if you show your love to my flesh, I shall again have to run my race. Please, then, do not seek to confer any greater favor upon me than that I be sacrificed to God while the altar is still prepared; that, being gathered together in love, you may sing praise to the Father, through Christ Jesus, that God has deemed me, the bishop of Syria, worthy to be summoned from the east unto the west. It is good to set from the world unto God, that I may rise again to him. . . .

I write to the churches, and impress on them all, that I shall willingly die for God, unless you hinder me. I beg you not to show an unseasonable goodwill towards me. Allow me to become food for the wild beasts, through whom it will be granted me to reach God. I am the wheat of God, and let me be ground by the teeth of the wild beasts, that I may be found the pure bread of Christ. Rather entice the wild beasts, that they may become my tomb, and may leave nothing of my body; so that when I have fallen asleep [in death], I may be no trouble to any one. Then shall I truly be a disciple of Christ, when the world shall not see so much as my body. Entreat Christ for me, that by these instruments I may be found a sacrifice [to God]. . . .

Though I am alive while I write to you, yet I am eager to die. My love has been crucified, and there is no fire in me desiring to be fed; but there is within me a water that lives and speaks, saying to me inwardly, "Come to the Father." I have no delight in corruptible food, nor in the pleasures of this life. I desire the bread of God, the heavenly bread, the bread of life, which is the flesh of Jesus Christ, the Son of God, who became afterwards of the seed of David and Abraham; and I desire the drink of God, namely his blood, which is incorruptible love and eternal life.[9]

—ST. IGNATIUS OF ANTIOCH,
Letter to the Romans 2, 4, 7

11

ST. IRENAEUS OF LYONS, BLESSED PEACEMAKER

ORN AND RAISED IN SMYRNA, ASIA MINOR (modern Turkey), St. Irenaeus, as a child, learned the faith from the great bishop St. Polycarp, who had in turn learned it from the Apostle John. So Irenaeus knew a day when the teaching of the Apostles was a living memory, and he learned the apostolic doctrine from a man who had learned it from the Apostles themselves.

Years later he would recall those days fondly. In a letter to another disciple of Polycarp, he wrote:

> I have a more vivid recollection of what occurred at that time than of recent events! . . . Polycarp used to sit and . . . speak of his familiar conversation with John, and with the rest of those who had seen the Lord; . . . he would call their words to remembrance, whatsoever he had heard from them about the Lord, with regard to his miracles and his teaching. Having received these things from the eyewitnesses of

the Word of life, Polycarp would recount them all
in harmony with the Scriptures. These things ... I
then listened to attentively, and stored them up not
on paper, but in my heart; and I am continually, by
God's grace, turning these things around accurately
in my mind.[1]

Indeed he did, to the end of his days, and he worked to
make sure the Apostles' doctrine would always remain a
living memory in the Church.

Something—we don't know what—drew young Irenaeus from his native place to the faraway city of Lugdu-
num in Gaul (modern-day Lyons, in France). There he
served as a priest and eventually as bishop.

It was a time of great creativity in the Church. Great
thinkers were making the first speculative explorations in
theology. New spiritual movements were rising up in every
corner of the known world. Having traveled so far, Irenaeus had experienced firsthand the great diversity of the
Church, and he loved it. Yet he also knew that not every
new development was truly Christian. His master Polycarp had warned about teachers who "pervert the oracles
of the Lord to their own desires"; he called such innovators
"the firstborn of Satan."[2]

Polycarp himself had once met the arch-heretic Marcion and addressed him as the "son of Satan." Marcion was
a fabulously wealthy shipbuilder who poured millions into
the spread of his strange Gospel. He preached that the

creator god was evil, as was the world he created, and that Jesus had come to set Christians free from bondage to this cruel tyrant. Since he detested the world, Marcion was also opposed to anything that could be construed as "good" in the world, including marriage, sex, and childbearing. These were merely the means by which the creator kept souls enslaved. Marcion considered the Old Testament to be diabolical, and he limited his "scriptures" to a much abridged and bowdlerized edition of Luke's Gospel and Paul's letters.

Nor was Marcionism the only upstart spiritual movement. Others arose in and around the cities of the empire, many of them sharing Marcion's contempt for creation. They tended to be elitist, offering salvation only for the few people who could understand their esoteric "knowledge." Since the Greek word for knowledge is *gnosis*, such movements became known as "Gnostic."

Irenaeus developed exceptionally sharp powers of discernment. He read widely in the works of these new movements, but he read the new works with eyes that had been trained by old Polycarp, whose own eyes had been trained by the Apostles.

He affirmed what he could in the new movements, and he tried his best to keep them Catholic. It was Irenaeus who persuaded one pope not to excommunicate the Montanists; an emerging movement that emphasized prophecy and moral rigor, the Montanists were attracting some of the leading lights of the time. It was Irenaeus who prevented an east-west schism by helping Pope Victor to understand the apostolic roots of the eastern churches' peculiar traditions for celebrating Easter.

The name *Irenaeus* means "peaceable," and St. Irenaeus lived up to the promise of his name. That was the judgment of the historian Eusebius (third century), who added that Irenaeus was "by temperament . . . a peacemaker," and that he "pleaded and negotiated thus for the peace of the churches."

Yet he would not buy peace at any cost. He would not compromise doctrine, and so he put forth heroic efforts to reason with wayward thinkers, to bring them around to the vicinities of truth. His greatest work is the sprawling five-volume *Adversus Haereses* ("Against the Heresies"), in which he takes on Gnosticism in all its many varieties. In Book 1, he lays out the Gnostic system and its history. In Book 2, he demonstrates that Gnostic claims are contrary to reason. In Book 3, he shows that Gnostic doctrines stand in stark contrast to the constant faith of the Church. In Book 4, he shows that they also contradict the sayings of Jesus. In Book 5, he homes in on the Gnostic denial of the resurrection of the flesh.

It's not a systematic treatise. It seems clear that he worked on it as time allowed, and Church life probably allowed him little time for writing projects. Yet it is all the more remarkable because it is so meandering; from the start of the work to its finish, Irenaeus remains utterly consistent and clear—and impressively simple and direct—in his exposition of Christian doctrine.

The Gnostics saw nothing but discord between spirit and matter. Irenaeus showed instead that these had been created in concord, but were later knocked askew by sin and finally restored by Christ.

The Gnostics perceived dissonance between the Old Testament and the New. Irenaeus demonstrated that the two testaments harmonized perfectly. Both, he said, "reveal one and the same God."[3] "One and the same householder produced both covenants, the Word of God, our Lord Jesus Christ, who spoke with both Abraham and Moses, and who has restored us anew to liberty, and has multiplied that grace which is from himself."[4] Giving readers a sweeping tour of salvation history, he showed "why more than one covenant was given to mankind, and what was the special character of each of these covenants."[5]

The bishop's tone varies as he wades through the Gnostic documents and examines their claims. Sometimes he speaks warmly. Other times he is driven to exasperation. At least once he resorts to satire, because the text before him is so absurd. But he kept at his task, because many souls were at stake.

In the end, he clearly and exhaustively demonstrated that we do not change gods as we move from the Old Testament to the New Testament. Nor does God change. But rather, God changes us as he shares the divine nature with his people (and that, incidentally, is what this book is about). We are transformed from slaves to sons and daughters, from followers of God's law to members of his faithful family, from people who fear to children who love.

Irenaeus knew that Scripture alone was insufficient as a guarantee of Christian faith. For, as Polycarp had pointed out, Scripture is not a self-interpreting text, and it is subject to the "inclinations" of the individual reader. Sometimes those inclinations are "perverse," and those whose inclinations are perverse are rarely able to admit their own perversity. It's possible even to say that they have good intentions.

But good intentions are not enough. Irenaeus insisted that all doctrinal development must be "in harmony with the Scriptures" (as it had been for Polycarp). It should harmonize as well with the prayer of the Church, especially as it is celebrated in the liturgy: "Our way of thinking," he said, "is attuned to the Eucharist, and the Eucharist in turn confirms our way of thinking."[6] It must, moreover, conform to the faith as it was kept everywhere: "the Catholic Church possesses one and the same faith throughout the whole world."[7]

That left no room whatsoever for elite groups of "knowers" or alternative "churches." In the Christian faith—as it had been established by the Apostles, and as it was kept in the Catholic Church—there could not be a "secret" knowledge reserved for a few while the rest mucked along with a carnal Gospel. There was one faith, and it was universal—that is, Catholic. Here comes everybody. Or, as one of the later Fathers put it: the apostolic faith is what has been taught always and everywhere and by everyone: all the saints.

For Irenaeus, the local bishop was the great guardian of the apostolic teaching for his Church. The bishop served as judge in the name of the Church and in the name of Christ. First among all the world's bishops was the bishop of Rome (see the extract that follows).

The test of Irenaeus's faith was his martyrdom. Few, if any, of the ancient Gnostics were willing to offer their lives as proof of their "knowledge." Irenaeus (like his master Polycarp) was just one of thousands of Catholics who gave their lives in testimony to their faith.

We know nothing more about the circumstances of his death, except that he has always been venerated as a martyr. Irenaeus would probably point out that the fact of his martyrdom is the only detail that matters.

PONDER IN YOUR HEART

Against the anarchy of Gnosticism, St. Irenaeus argued for the necessity and usefulness of the papal office.

All, therefore, who wish to see the Truth, can view in every Church the tradition of the Apostles which has been manifested in the whole world. Besides, we are able to list the bishops who were appointed in the Churches by the Apostles, and their lines of successors even to ourselves. These neither taught nor knew of anything like what the heretics rave about ...

Since, however, in a volume of this kind it would be very long to count up the lines of succession of all the Churches, we point out the tradition, received from the Apostles, as well as the faith preached to men, which has come down even to us through the lines of succession of the bishops, namely, that of the chief and most ancient Church, known to all, which was founded and built up at Rome by the two most glorious Apostles, Peter and Paul. In this way we put to confusion all those who in any way whatever, either because of an evil self-complacency, or of vainglory, or of blindness and evil-mindedness, gather in unauthorized assemblies. The reason is this: with this Church it is necessary that every Church, that is, the faithful who are everywhere, should be in agreement, because of her greater sovereignty; in which the apostolic tradition has always been safeguarded by those who are everywhere.

The blessed Apostles, therefore, having founded and built up the Church, handed over to Linus the bishopric for administrating the Church ... [*Here follows the complete list of popes down to Irenaeus's day.*] ... And this is the fullest proof that there is one and the

same life-giving faith, which has been safeguarded
in the Church from the Apostles till now and has
been handed down in truth.[8]

—ST. IRENAEUS OF LYONS,
Against the Heresies 3.3.1–3

12

ST. JEROME AND HIS CIRCLE

W E DIE ALONE. WE ARE JUDGED ON OUR own fidelity and not the faithfulness of those around us. But along the way to a happy death we must live a life, as human nature dictates, *in society*. Some of us have an easier time of it than others.

St. Jerome had an easy time of it—sometimes. And sometimes he didn't. There is something edifying and beautiful about his friendships with other canonized saints. Yet there is something sobering about his enmity toward still other canonized saints. Here I plan to concentrate mostly on his friendships, though his quarrels will inevitably intrude.

His primary friendship was with Jesus. Brilliant as he was—multilingual, well read in the classics, and a prodigious writer—Jerome had a simple piety. He wanted to know Jesus more deeply. It was Jerome who famously said, "Ignorance of Scripture is ignorance of Christ."[1]

No one could accuse him of such ignorance—or any sort of ignorance, really.

St. Jerome grew up in the remote provincial city of Stridon (in what is now Croatia). His parents must have recognized that he was a genius, and they sent him off to study in Rome during his teen years. He studied under some of the imperial capital's great minds, and he wasted a lot of time, too. But at some point (probably around age nineteen) he decided to take his Christian faith seriously. He leaned into his studies, and on Sundays he and his friends would go out to the Roman catacombs to walk the dark corridors amid the exposed remains of the ancient saints.

On completing his studies he resolved to give his life entirely to Christ. He returned to his homeland and gathered a community of like-minded young ascetics. Their common life didn't last long. Jerome had an irascible temperament, and he could be as demanding of others as he was of himself. And though he had learned many things in Rome, diplomacy was not one of them.

With a friend he continued his experiments in asceticism, traveling to the east. In Antioch he polished his knowledge of Greek and began to study Hebrew, all to enhance his study of the Sacred Page. Then he took to the Syrian desert for two years of living as a hermit. There he gained renown for both his asceticism and his erudition. A bishop of Antioch eventually recruited Jerome to be his theological advisor—and also ordained him to the priesthood. Jerome accompanied his bishop to the great Council of Constantinople in 381 and then followed him to business in Rome.

St. Damasus was then pope, and he soon recognized the young visitor's genius. He invited him to stay as papal secretary. Damasus also noticed Jerome's love for Scripture, and he commissioned his secretary to produce a much-needed revision of the Latin Church's common translation of the Bible, called the Vulgate. Jerome eagerly took up the project, renewing his studies in Hebrew under a Roman rabbi.

When in Rome, he attracted other notice as well. Some of his fellow clergymen resented his brusqueness, envied his accomplishments, and sometimes saw his asceticism as a reproach to their own soft lives.

These same qualities, however, gained the attention of Romans who wanted to pursue a more demanding spiritual life. Some decades earlier, St. Athanasius had visited the city and introduced the ideals of Egyptian monasticism. This had instilled in certain Roman noblewomen a deep desire to live that way. In one household after another, widowed matrons were turning their rooms over to this purpose and dedicating their days to prayer and poverty, fasting and works of charity.

In Jerome these matrons found a kindred spirit, and they sought him out as a spiritual director, a role he was eager to assume. But he required that the households add another dimension to their regimen. He insisted that they take up biblical studies.

Nor were these "soft" Bible studies, where attendees

were asked to express their feelings about select Scripture passages. Rather, Jerome tutored large classes of women in the fine points of Hebrew philology. Their questions pushed him further in his studies and provoked him to compose word studies in response. Soon they were chanting the Psalms in Hebrew as part of the daily devotions they prayed in common. And Jerome was lamenting that they had surpassed him in their ability to speak Hebrew without an accent!

There was not a bishop alive who could speak the language of the Old Testament, but Jerome was teaching it to Roman widows and teenagers.

One of the matrons, Marcella, was inclined to linguistic study, and so she drew out Jerome's expositions of the literal sense of the biblical texts. A younger widow, Paula, favored allegorical readings, and Jerome was just as willing and able to provide those. Paula's daughters would follow her in the ascetical life, one as a consecrated virgin and another as a widow. The virgin, Eustochium, would serve as Jerome's secretary and research assistant for most of the remainder of his life.

As Jerome gave spiritual direction to this circle of consecrated women, it seems that they also helped to form *his* character, perhaps moderating his temper now and then. He writes in one letter to Marcella: "I know that as you read these words you will knit your brows, and fear that my freedom of speech is sowing the seeds of fresh quarrels; and that, if you could, you would gladly put your finger over my mouth to prevent me from even speaking of things which others do not blush to do."[2] No doubt, Marcella had had occasions to silence her teacher in the past. He respected her judgment, and he welcomed the help.

Nevertheless, Jerome and his companions became the subject of gossip among envious and irritated clergymen. Jerome left Rome under some sense of compulsion. But his exodus itself became an occasion of grace for his disciples; they decided to accompany him on a pilgrimage to the Holy Land, to study the Bible in its native place.

Arriving at their destination, the pilgrims chose to settle there. They raised a complex of monasteries near the place where Jesus was born: monasteries for men, for women, and for Christians of every social class. And there they continued their research and publications for decades. Nearby was the library of Caesarea—probably the world's greatest collection for biblical studies—the library that had been founded by Origen and supplemented by Eusebius.

Jerome himself conducted biblical scholarship to rival all the authors in that library combined! He wrote commentaries, translations, polemics, controversial works, and many letters. He compiled reference works on all the place names and all the personal names in the Bible.

His circle stayed with him. (Alas, so did his feuds.) He pushed his friends forward, and they pushed him. He comforted them when they were troubled. They eased his ill tempers, too.

As they drew closer in friendship, they drew one

another more deeply into God's word, more deeply into the mystery, more deeply into friendship with Christ. And they drew the whole world with them.

PONDER IN YOUR HEART

Jerome took the heretic Vigilantius to task for rejecting the Church's devotion to the saints. This passage is pure Jerome, with his characteristic rhetorical flourishes, frequent biblical allusions, and vitriol.

The truth is that the saints are not called dead, but are said to be asleep. This is why Lazarus, who was about to rise again, is said to have slept (John 11:11). And the Apostle forbids the Thessalonians to be sorry for those who were asleep (1 Thessalonians 4:13). As for you, when wide awake you are asleep, and asleep when you write, and you bring before me an apocryphal book which, under the name of Ezra, is read by you and those of your ilk, and in this book it is written that after death no one dares pray for others. I have never read the book: for what need is there to take up what the Church does not receive? ... I say this because in your short treatise you quote Solomon as if he were on your side, though Solomon never wrote the words in question at all; so that, as you have a second Ezra you may have a second Solomon. And, if you like, you may read the imaginary revelations of all the patriarchs and prophets, and, when you have learned them, you may sing them among the women in their weaving-shops, or rather order them to be read in your taverns, the more easily by these melancholy ditties to stimulate the ignorant mob to replenish their cups.

As to the question of candles, however, we do not, as you in vain misrepresent us, light them in the daytime, but by their solace we would cheer the darkness of the night, and watch for the dawn, lest we should be blind like you and sleep in darkness. And if some persons ... adopt the practice in honor of the martyrs, what harm is thereby done to you? Once upon a time even the Apostles pleaded that the ointment was wasted, but they were rebuked by the voice of the Lord. Christ did not need the ointment, nor do martyrs need the light of candles; and yet that woman poured out the ointment in honor of Christ, and her heart's devotion was accepted. All those who light these candles have their reward according to their faith ...

Does the bishop of Rome do wrong when he offers sacrifices to the Lord over the venerable bones of the dead men Peter and Paul, as we should say—but according to you, over a worthless bit of dust—and judges their tombs worthy to be Christ's altars? And not only is the bishop of one city in error, but the bishops of the whole world, who, despite the tavern-keeper Vigilantius, enter the basilicas of the dead, in which a worthless bit of dust and ashes lies wrapped up in a cloth, defiled and defiling all else. Thus, according to you, the sacred buildings are like the sepulchers of the Pharisees, whitened without, while within they have filthy remains, and are full of foul smells and uncleanliness. And then he dares to expectorate his filth upon the subject and to say: Is it the case that the souls of the martyrs love their ashes, and hover round them, and are always present, lest haply if any one come to pray and they were absent, they could not hear?

Oh, monster, who ought to be banished to the ends of the earth! Do you laugh at the relics of the martyrs, and in company with Eunomius, the father of this heresy, slander the churches of Christ? Are you not afraid of being in such company, and of speaking against us the same things that he utters against the Church? ... I am surprised you do not tell us that there must be no martyrdoms, inasmuch as God, who does not ask for the blood of goats and bulls, much less requires the blood of men. This is what you say, or rather, even if you do not say it, you are taken as meaning to assert it. For in maintaining that the relics of the martyrs are to be trodden under foot, you forbid the shedding of their blood as being worthy of no honor.[3]

—St. Jerome, *Against Vigilantius* 6–8

13

ST. MONICA AND HER SON

THERE'S A YIDDISH PROVERB YOU'LL FIND quoted in many books on parenting: "Little children disturb your sleep; big children your life."

St. Monica of Thagaste could corroborate that claim and commiserate with the best of modern parents. Her eldest child, Augustine, disturbed her sleep in the normal course of events—and then went on to disturb seventeen years of her life.

Augustine's youth was a trial for his devout mother. She had raised him as a Christian, though her husband, Patrick, was not a believer. She had made sure he received a Christian education, and she herself set a good example. Though Monica probably could not read, she attended Mass daily so that she could hear the Word of God proclaimed, and she even attended all her parish funerals, so that she could hear the Gospel a second time.

All the best training, however, could not ensure a child's fidelity. Her son spent his teen years causing trouble in the neighborhood—pilfering pears from the neighbor's grove, just for the thrill of rebellion.

As he went from high school to college (the fourth-century equivalents, anyway), he moved from the town of Thagaste to the big city of Carthage—and from bad to worse. He took a mistress and got her pregnant. He stopped going to church and expressed contempt for the lowbrow quality of the Scriptures. They seemed primitive and boorish compared to the trendy philosophy and polished rhetoric he was studying at school.

Still worse, he began to dabble in heresy. The eastern cult of the Manichees was all the rage among urban intellectuals at the time. It was syncretistic, a patchwork of doctrines from several world religions, including Christianity but also Buddhism and Zoroastrianism. Its adherents claimed that their doctrine was completely rational and required no faith. What's more, they sneered at the Bible stories that had so bothered Augustine. Like the Gnostics before them, they opposed the Old Testament God; they despised his worship; and they considered themselves to be prisoners in his creation. Yet they also kept a veneer of Christianity: a professed esteem for Jesus as a prophet, a doctrine that emphasized salvation, and a "church" that was governed by "bishops."

Augustine didn't embrace Manicheism. He never signed on as one of the "elect." Rather he was a "hearer." He studied it, and though it didn't quite make sense to him, he assumed the problem was with his own limitations or the limitations of his local teachers. He hung on any-way, placing himself at the service of the "elect" and await-ing the day he could converse with one of the movement's leading intellectuals.

Such circumstances were the cause of Monica's heart-break: her son had taken up heresy, served a bizarre cult, and now lived in sin with a mistress. Though his profes-sional prestige soared, she could not take delight in it. His own pride in his accomplishments only exacerbated his condition. When she asked her bishop for help, he told her that Augustine wasn't ready to be helped—he was far too proud.

Monica tried to control the damage. She urged her son, at least, not to commit adultery—not to sleep with mar-ried women. She made the moral case persuasively. And, he took her advice, showing that, for all his self-regard, he still respected her wisdom. He went a step further: though he never married his mistress, he remained faithful to her.

Augustine eventually grew disillusioned with the Man-ichees. He had his chance to meet with one of their leading lights, a bishop named Faustus, but the man was unable to answer Augustine's probing questions.

Still, Augustine drew no closer to Christianity. He turned instead to Neo-Platonist philosophy, which was Greco-Roman paganism's last, best hope.

Monica prayed more passionately. She complained to God with tears and expressed her disappointment—and even anger—about heaven's seeming silence. She spent long hours haunting chapels, keeping vigil. And she kept this up for seventeen years!

In his *Confessions*, Augustine describes what would prove to be the turning point of his life. It began with his journey from North Africa to Milan in 384. He had been appointed to the most prestigious academic position in the Latin world as professor of rhetoric at the imperial court. Monica, by then a widow, decided to accompany him.

In Milan he was attracted by the reputation of the Christian Church's great bishop, St. Ambrose—who happened also to be Monica's spiritual director. Notable for his own accomplishments, Ambrose had served as governor of the empire's de facto capital before he was brought to Church office by acclamation of the people. He was a man of formidable intellectual and rhetorical skills.

Augustine recalls that Ambrose's renown extended "throughout the world," and the young scholar determined "to judge for myself whether the reports of his powers as a speaker were accurate." Perhaps the upstart was checking out the competition or measuring his own gifts against those of his elders.

In any event, he was surprised at what he found. He was attracted first by Ambrose's warmth and humility. Then, unexpectedly, he found himself drawn by Ambrose's teaching: "every Sunday I listened as he preached the word of truth to the people, and I grew more and more certain that it was possible to unravel the tangle woven by those who had deceived both me and others with their cunning lies against the Holy Scriptures."

Gradually Augustine discovered that he had judged the Scriptures unfairly and inaccurately, misunderstanding their genres and the Church's interpretive methods. Ambrose's preaching showed him "how to interpret the ancient Scriptures of the law and the prophets in a different light from that which had previously made them seem absurd, when I used to criticize your saints for holding beliefs which they had never really held at all. I was pleased to hear that in his sermons to the people Ambrose often repeated the text: 'The written law inflicts death, whereas the spiritual law brings life' [2 Corinthians 3:6], as though this were a rule upon which he wish to insist most carefully. And when he lifted the veil of mystery and disclosed the spiritual meaning of texts ... I was not aggrieved by what he said."

A worldly intellectual who once sneered at the uncouth rusticity of the Old Testament, Augustine soon came to profess that "the Scriptures were delivered to mankind by the Spirit of the one true God who can tell no lie." Moreover, he held that "it was precisely this," and not any fine points of philosophical theory, that he "most needed to believe."

And then he provided his trademark gloss on the matter: "since we are too weak to discover the truth by reason alone," he explained, God "invested the Bible" with "conspicuous authority" so that it could "be the means by which we should look for" God and believe in him. What he had previously judged to be absurd stories, he now regarded as "profound mysteries." He concluded that "the authority of Scripture should be respected and accepted with the purest faith, because while all can read it with ease, it also has a deeper meaning in which its great secrets are locked away."

At first attracted by the humble warmth of Ambrose, Augustine was converted by the profound humility of God, who cloaked his divine word in such homely attire— all so that he might draw "so great a throng in the embrace of its holy humility."

It was a faith his mother, in her own humility, had always loved—even when God seemed slow in answering her prayers.

Through the rest of his *Confessions*, Augustine presents his mother as the model Christian, the model saint—the model of a life lived in union with God. He said of Monica: "To her I owe all that I am."

God had answered Monica's prayers in a way that was best not only for her son, and not only for her, but for all humanity through all the future years of its history. Augustine went on to become a bishop who reconciled entire congregations of heretics to the Catholic faith—Manichees, Donatists, Pelagians, and many others. He would not have been so effective if he had not had firsthand experience of heresy—if he had not known it from the inside.

Nor could he have taught the Church to appreciate the Scriptures so deeply if he had not once held them in contempt.

God does not will that any of us should ever sin. Yet his will is accomplished in spite of our sins, and even through our sins. As St. Paul put it, "We know that in everything God works for good with those who love him, who are called according to his purpose" (Romans 8:28).

St. Augustine disturbed years of his mother's life, but God put those years to good use, and we're all the beneficiaries.

PONDER IN YOUR HEART

At the culmination of his monumental work, The City of God, *St. Augustine explains the intercessory power of the saints in heaven.*

To what do these miracles witness, but to this faith that preaches Christ risen in the flesh, and ascended with the same flesh into heaven? For the martyrs themselves were *martyrs*—that is to say, "witnesses" of this faith—drawing upon themselves by their testimony the hatred of the world. They conquered the world not by resisting it, but by dying. For this faith they died, and can now ask these benefits from the Lord, for whose name they were slain. For this faith their marvelous constancy was exercised, so that in these miracles great power was manifested as the result. For if the resurrection of the flesh to eternal life had not taken place in Christ, and were not to be accomplished in his people—as predicted by Christ himself, or by the prophets who foretold that Christ was to come—why do the martyrs who were slain for this faith, which proclaims the resurrection, possess such power?

For God himself may work these miracles by that wonderful manner of working by which he produces effects in time, though he remains eternal. Or he may work them through servants—and, if so, he may make use of the spirits of martyrs as he uses men who are still in the body, or even work all these marvels by means of angels, over whom he exerts an invisible, immutable, incorporeal sway.

What is said to be done by the martyrs, then, is done not by their working, but only by their prayer and request . . .

Our martyrs are not our gods; for we know that we and the martyrs have but one and the same God . . . [The pagans] built temples to their gods, and set up altars, and ordained priests, and appointed sacrifices; but to our martyrs we build not temples, as if they were gods, but monuments as to dead men whose spirits live with God. Neither do we erect altars at these monuments that we may sacrifice to the martyrs, but to the one God shared by the martyrs and ourselves; and in this sacrifice they are named in their own place and rank as men of God who conquered the world by confessing him, but they are not invoked by the sacrificing priest. For it is to God, not to them, that he sacrifices, though he sacrifices at their monument; for he is God's priest, not theirs. The sacrifice itself, too, is the Body of Christ, which is not offered to them, because *they themselves are this body!* . . .

—ST. AUGUSTINE OF HIPPO,
City of God 22.9–10

14

ST. THOMAS AQUINAS,
BIBLICAL THEOLOGIAN

S T. THOMAS AQUINAS IS REVERED AND RE-
spected more than he is loved today, and that's because he is often misunderstood. He was indeed a
great champion of reason. He was a man whose philosophy
was expressed in language precisely technical and plod-
dingly comprehensive.

For all this, however, he was *not* a rationalist, as some
of his detractors would have us believe. He was *not* simply Aristotle dressed up in priestly vestments. And he was
definitely *not* a bore.

He was a priest of the thirteenth century, a member of
the newly established Order of Preachers, the Dominicans.
He was descended from the aristocracy of southern Italy.
He was quiet and inclined to scholarly research and writing. For many years he taught theology at the University of
Paris. He was a prolific writer, keeping multiple secretaries
busy simultaneously with his dictation. He produced thousands of words per day of his adult life. His most famous

work is his great, unfinished *Summa Theologica*, perhaps the most comprehensive systematic account of Christian theology ever attempted.

A quiet, humble man, he had epic and holy ambitions. In order to achieve them, he needed to observe the rigorous disciplines of philosophical theology—he had to be passionate about a language that very few people find exciting.

Still, I believe that St. Thomas is best understood not simply by looking at his metaphysics or by studying his appropriation of Aristotle. Rather I suggest that St. Thomas is fundamentally a *biblical* theologian. In fact, many of his biographers tell us that Thomas would have described himself primarily as a teacher of Scripture.

One of Thomas's earliest biographers, the Dominican Bernard Gui, wrote (during Thomas's canonization process, c. 1318), "His knowledge was like an overflowing river of scriptural doctrine, sprung from the fount of Wisdom on high and then branching out through all the variety of his writings."[1]

Many scholars now are rediscovering the biblical depth of his teachings and the importance of appropriating the scriptural categories that formed the framework of much of his thought. Today he is recognized by many as one of the greatest biblical theologians in history.

As St. Thomas himself says, "Our faith receives its surety from Scripture." Why is Scripture so uniquely authoritative? St. Thomas answers: "Because the author of

Sacred Scripture is God, in Whose power it is to accommodate not only words for expressing things, which even man is able to do, *but also the things themselves.*"

God "writes" the world, then, the way people write words. Thus, nature and history are more than just created things; they have more than just a literal, historical meaning. God fashions the things of the world and shapes the events of history as visible signs of other, uncreated realities, which are eternal and invisible. St. Thomas says, "As words formed by man are signs of his intellectual knowledge, so are creatures formed by God signs of his wisdom."

But because of sin's blinding effects, the "book" of nature must be translated by the inspired Word of Scripture. Nature, since the fall, cannot be truly understood apart from Scriptures.

This is precisely the view taken in the *Catechism of the Catholic Church* (see nn. 112 and 116), where the Magisterium refers us to the interpretive approach of St. Thomas.

Apart from Scriptures, not even such a genius as St. Thomas could have made much sense of God's purpose for salvation history. And Thomas knew that.

Consider his *Treatise on Law.* That treatise is interesting because, like many sections of the *Summa*, it quotes Aristotle often. But, when you total up the number of quotations, you find that 724 quotations are from Scripture and only 96 from Aristotle. I believe this reveals the supremely important place of Scripture in St. Thomas's understanding of law.

Thomas deals with the meaning of law in Question 90. He defines it as an ordinance of reason promulgated for the common good, made by one who has care for the community. But he goes on to explain that law is that which guides man to his end. The point is simple. We were made for God but, because of sin, we need divine assistance. Law raises God's children to the heights of Trinitarian glory.

He goes on to explain four types of law: *eternal law*, which represents God's governance of creation; *natural law*, which is man's participation in the eternal law, and through which, by our reason and by our free will, we come to know what is true and choose what is good; and *human law*, which applies the general principles of natural law to particular periods and situations for the common good of society.

But I am most interested in the fourth type: *divine law*. Divine law is the law that God has revealed to us for a truly unique purpose. If the end of human law is the promotion of the common good among men, the divine law has for its purpose nothing less than our friendship with God.

Divine law is necessary for God's own fatherly purposes to be known and realized. In divine law, we discover that we were made for something greater than earthly happiness and temporal goods. We were made for the beatific vision, participation in the very life and blessedness of the Trinity for all eternity.

But how does God get us there? Our nature was never enough to gain us supernatural life, even before the Fall. Original Sin only made matters worse. Because of our imperfection and sinfulness, the divine law had to be delivered in two stages, the Old Law and the New Law (i.e., the Old and New Covenants).

Have you ever noticed that the Old Testament doesn't talk about the resurrection or heaven very much, if at all? Why not? Because in the Old Law, God gave us what we wanted—temporal welfare, prosperity, and power—in order to prepare us for the revelation of what we really needed and were made for—divine life and heavenly glory.

If diplomacy is the art of letting someone else have *your* way, then God is the consummate diplomat. St. Thomas explains that the promises of the Old Law concern temporal goods because of sin. For God to get us back where we could attain our supernatural glory, he first had to restore a bond of trust between himself and us. As the people of Israel attained these material goods, they discovered over time that ultimately the goods of earth are signs that point to the everlasting goods of heaven. Thus, when Jesus came proclaiming the New Law, it's the law of the kingdom, but it's no longer merely an earthly kingdom.

The Old Law is designed with our fallen human condition in mind, getting us ready for the New Law, which is given to us by Jesus Christ. The Old Law, St. Thomas explains, is an intermediate step between the natural law and the New Law. Apart from the Old Law, man didn't know he had a supernatural end. With it, man learned he had a supernatural end to hope for, but he still lacked the means or strength to achieve it.

The New Law—the Gospel of Jesus Christ—is what delivers to man the power needed to keep the divine law as well as the natural law. St. Thomas goes so far as to identify the New Law with the indwelling presence of the Holy Spirit in the heart of the baptized believer who lives in a state of grace as a son or daughter of the living God.

Thus, for Aquinas, the New Law goes beyond the Sermon on the Mount and the other teachings of Jesus. It is nothing less than divine grace—divine life and power. Grace *is* the New Law that enables us to keep the commandments in a way that we as children of Adam couldn't on our own.

In his *Treatise on Law*, Thomas presents the Gospel the same way the Magisterium of the Church has presented it for two thousand years. The divine law is given in order to humble—and then exalt—us. First the Old Law humbled us and showed us our weakness and hence our need for grace. Then the New Law exalted us by filling us with the Holy Spirit.

If we understand this approach, we will see how inescapable the theological dimension of law is to St. Thomas and how essential divine grace is for us to keep both the natural law and the New Law.

Where does all this begin for the Catholic who wants to understand the Scriptures, but has no time to study at the University of Paris? It begins for you and me where it began for St. Thomas Aquinas. We begin, as he did, on our knees, with Bible in hand.

Said Bernard Gui in praising the habits of our hero: "O wondrous mystery of Providence, that at first God conceals the meaning of his Scripture and then at last reveals it, in order to show how far short of his mysteries comes human understanding and that whoever desires the least insight into them must have recourse to him who chose to reveal his secrets to the Prophets and the Apostles!

"O happy soul whose prayer was heard by God in his mercy, who thus teaches us, by this example, to possess our questioning souls in patience, so that in the study of divine things we rely chiefly on the power of prayer!"

PONDER IN YOUR HEART

St. Thomas searched the Scriptures in order to understand the blessed afterlives of the saints in heaven.

The soul that is beatified by the vision of God is made one with him in understanding. The knower and the known must somehow be one. And so, when God reigns in the saints, they too reign along with God. In their person are uttered the words of the Apocalypse 5:10: "(You have) made them a kingdom and priests to our God, and they shall reign on earth." This kingdom, in which God reigns in the saints and the saints reign with God, is called the kingdom of heaven, according to Matthew 3:2:

"Repent, for the kingdom of heaven is at hand." This is the same manner of speaking as that whereby presence in heaven is ascribed to God, not in the sense that He is housed in the material heavens, but to show forth the eminence of God over every creature, in the way that heaven towers high above every other material creature, as is indicated in Psalm 112:4: "The Lord is high above all nations, and his glory above the heavens!" . . .

The ultimate good we have been speaking of contains perpetual and full joy. Our Lord was thinking of this when he bade us, in John 16:24: "Ask and you will receive, that your joy may be full." Full joy, however, can be gained from no creature, but only from God, in whom the entire plenitude of goodness resides. And so our Lord says to the faithful servant in Matthew 25:21: "enter into the joy of your master," that you may have the joy of your Lord, as is indicated in Job 22:26: "then you will delight yourself in the Almighty." Since God rejoices most of all in himself, the faithful servant is said to enter into the joy of his Lord inasmuch as he enters into the joy wherein his Lord rejoices, as our Lord said on another occasion, when he made a promise to his disciples: "and I assign to you, as my Father assigned to me, a kingdom, that you may eat and drink at my table in my kingdom" (Luke 22:29ff.). Not that the saints, once they have been made incorruptible, have any use for bodily foods in that final state of good; no, by the table is meant rather the replenishment of joy that God has in himself and that the saints have from him.

—ST. THOMAS AQUINAS,
Compendium of Theology, n. 165

15

ST. THERESE OF LISIEUX, SAINT OF LITTLE THINGS

NLIKE MOSES AND ST. PAUL, ST. THERESE of Lisieux was not, in her lifetime, a player on the world stage. Nor was she a great scholar like Jerome or an original thinker like Augustine. She did not hold high office, as Irenaeus did. She did not die dramatically as a martyr for the faith, as Ignatius did. She did not synthesize great systems of thought, as Thomas did.

Her prodigy was her littleness—and, paradoxically, her littleness is so large that it can be frightening. For no other chapter in this book have I been so intimidated. For no other chapter have I stared so long at a blank page. All the saints should inspire awe in us, but for most of them we can get around our awe by reciting their résumé. Not so with Therese. She doesn't have much of a résumé.

She died at age twenty-four, having spent nine years behind the walls of a Carmelite cloister. She passed her days, mostly, with prayer and menial tasks. She fell to tuberculosis, as did millions of other people in 1897. When she died, she left behind little more than a small bundle of notebooks. Even among her sisters in the cloister, she did not stand out. One nun who lived with her summed her up, posthumously, as "good for nothing."

But just a few years after she died—and many years before she was canonized—Pope St. Pius X called her "the greatest saint of modern times." Pope Pius XI, who canonized her in 1925, spoke of her as "the star of his pontificate." Pope Pius XII held that she was "the greatest healer of modern times." Blessed Pope John Paul II named her one of the thirty-three "Doctors of the Church"—the elite saints who stand out for the superlative quality of their teaching.

No praise of Therese is so intimidating to me as the line addressed to her by Pope John Paul I: "Therese, the love you bore God . . . was truly worthy of him."

What happened after 1897 to elevate this "good for nothing," unproductive life to the ranks of the most exemplary?

It was the publication of her notebooks in 1898 as the spiritual memoir *Story of a Soul*, which she had written under obedience from her superiors.

The *Story* begins with a happy early childhood in a loving home, presided over by two pious bourgeois parents: Louis and Zelie Martin. (They would become, in 2008, the first husband and wife beatified as a couple.) Therese's father (like mine) was a jeweler. Her mother was a successful lace maker. Eventually her father gave up his own trade in order to devote himself to his wife's business. The Martins had nine children, four of whom died in infancy or early childhood. The five who survived to adulthood, all daughters, became nuns. Therese was the youngest of these, an intelligent, impetuous little girl, tending to emotional extremes.

When Therese was just four years old, her mother died from breast cancer. Therese turned inward. Her sister Pauline, then barely sixteen years old, became like a second mother for her, but Therese grieved again when Pauline entered the convent.

Therese never felt she fit in at school. She was bullied. And she lived for the time she spent at home with her family. From an early age, she discerned a vocation to become a Carmelite nun. She even sought, unsuccessfully, a dispensation so that she could enter the monastery as a child. On a pilgrimage to Rome, she created quite a scene when she threw herself at the feet of Pope Leo XIII and begged him to grant her the dispensation. Refusing to get up, she was dragged away by the Swiss Guards.

Her inner life, though, was hardly simple. By her own account, she was oppressed by sadness and self-absorbed. She fantasized about performing heroic religious deeds—traveling to distant lands as a missionary, dying as a martyr, and so on. But she was also plagued by scruples over the gravity of her perceived faults and sins.

She experienced a healing, a conversion of sorts, on Christmas Eve when she was thirteen, and she attributed it to the kindness of the baby Jesus. For Therese, it was a turn away from a persistent, unnatural sadness toward a more childlike acceptance of God's grace, love, and mercy. How beautiful that the moment arrived just as her childhood was coming to an end.

She was permitted to enter the cloister a little early, at age fifteen. Leaving the world behind, she still took many of her illusions with her. She was ambitious to achieve recognizably heroic sanctity, and she pursued this—without any sense of success—for six years!

It was then that she had a sort of second conversion. It was a discovery. She spoke of it in terms of new technology:

> You know it has ever been my desire to become a saint, but I have always felt, in comparing myself with the saints, that I am as far removed from them as the grain of sand, which the passer-by tramples underfoot, is remote from the mountain whose summit is lost in the clouds.
>
> Instead of being discouraged, I concluded that God would not inspire desires which could not be realized, and that I may aspire to sanctity in spite of my littleness. For me to become great is impossible. I must bear with myself and my many imperfections; but I will seek out a means of getting to heaven by a little way—very short and very straight, a little way that is wholly new.

We live in an age of inventions; nowadays the rich need not trouble to climb the stairs, they have elevators instead. Well, I mean to try and find an elevator by which I may be raised unto God, for I am too tiny to climb the steep stairway of perfection.[1]

She searched the Scriptures for clues and happened upon this line, from the Vulgate rendering of the Book of Proverbs: "Whosoever is a little one, let him come to me" (Proverbs 9:4). She found this invitation confirmed in the oracles of the Prophet Isaiah (see Isaiah 66:12) and, of course, by Jesus: "Unless you turn and become like children, you will not enter the kingdom of heaven" (Matthew 18:2).

Ever after she used the word *little* often in describing her efforts. It was not a pejorative. It would become, in the words of later commentators, her way of spiritual childhood. Or, as she herself, put it: her "little way."

This was no license for her to slacken her ambitions or shirk what she formerly considered duties. Quite the opposite. She still kept to the same regimen, which was standard for nuns in the cloister. She still faced the same tasks. The difference was that she approached them with the joy of a child at play, confident in her Father's love and tender care.

I don't mean to say her suffering ended. She contracted tuberculosis and endured pain, sickness, and incapacity that I don't have the strength to imagine. Moreover, she underwent a time of trial when she found it difficult to believe the promises of faith. The thought of heaven, which had long been a comfort, became sheer torment. She felt it necessary to copy out the creed and carry it with her at all times. She described the experience as a "dark tunnel" she had to walk through to get to the light. Yet through it all, she trusted the Father. She entrusted him with her care, her salvation, and her ability to endure the ordeal. She trusted God to take her by the hand and get her safely to the other side. She had no reason to doubt his desire to do so.

Very few of her fellow nuns knew the magnitude of her suffering, because she endured it with such good cheer. And it wasn't only in the great matters of the ravages of tuberculosis. She accepted the annoyances of those around her—one nun's habit of clacking her beads together during the recitation of the Rosary—and even came to love such moments. The nun who most annoyed Therese believed herself to be the little saint's most intimate friend.

After her death, her blood sisters (who were also with her in the convent) collected passages from her various notebooks and brought them out in a book, expecting it to be a memento of interest mostly to family members. It became a publishing phenomenon, soon translated into dozens of languages and selling millions of copies.

In all the history of Christianity, few books have been

so influential. No author, not even the great popes, have had such a profound impact on the development of spirituality in the last century.

Hers is a "little way," but a way that we all could walk. If only we let go of our pretenses of adulthood—control, self-determination, self-pity, and bluster. If only we will.

PONDER IN YOUR HEART

Therese offered these words of encouragement to a seminarian in 1897, the last year of her life.

Sometimes, when I read books in which perfection is put before us with the goal obstructed by a thousand obstacles, my poor little head is quickly fatigued. I close the learned treatise, which tires my brain and dries up my heart, and I turn to the Sacred Scriptures. Then all becomes clear and lightsome—a single word opens out infinite vistas, perfection appears easy, and I see that it is enough to acknowledge our nothingness, and like children surrender ourselves into the Arms of the Good God. Leaving to great and lofty minds the beautiful books which I cannot understand, still less put in practice, I rejoice in my littleness because "only little children and those who are like them shall be admitted to the Heavenly banquet" (see Matthew 19:14). Fortunately—"there are many rooms in my Father's House" (see John 14:2): if there were only those—to me—incomprehensible mansions with their baffling roads, I should certainly never enter there.[2]

16

ST. MAXIMILIAN KOLBE, SAINT OF AUSCHWITZ

BIOGRAPHIES OF ST. MAXIMILIAN KOLBE usually begin at the end, or very near the end.

They begin at the Auschwitz death camp, the very image of murderous, godless despair—a place where four million people would be liquidated during the years of the Nazi occupation of Poland. The biographies always begin there, and begin at the moment when one man stepped forward to offer himself in a pure act of sacrificial, life-giving love.

Ten men had been chosen to die a slow, torturous death in the pit of Auschwitz, the starvation bunker. One of those men dropped to his knees and begged for mercy, for the sake of his wife and children.

And St. Maximilian Kolbe broke ranks, stepping forward and offering to die in place of the pleading man. Asked to identify himself, St. Maximilian—prisoner number 16670—uttered the last words we know to have come from his lips: "I am a Catholic priest."

If that were the whole of his life, it would be enough. But it was merely the final movement in a masterwork. Such sanctity is not built in a day. That moment was the fruit of a lifetime of love. Ultimately, as St. Maximilian might say, it was the fruit of an eternal love.

Born in Poland in 1894, Raymond Kolbe was mischievous and energetic, a difficult child who exasperated his mother. One day she was at wit's end. After punishing him yet again, she said to him, "Raymond, what will become of you?"

For some reason, the question made him pensive. He ran off to his parish church to put the question before the Blessed Virgin: "What will become of me?"

The Blessed Virgin appeared to him and, in answer to his question, offered him two crowns: one red, symbolizing martyrdom, the other white, symbolizing virginity. He responded that he would choose both.

Raymond returned home and told his mother, who came to believe him without any reservation, because of the radical transformation she witnessed in his character. Her troublemaker had vanished.

Soon afterward, Raymond, at age thirteen, entered the seminary of the Conventual Franciscans. He was still a high-energy youth, but now his energy was directed toward noble ends. He was inquisitive, with a fertile mind. He devoured books of physics and even set down the design of a rocket for space exploration. In religion he would take the name Maximilian.

The Franciscan superiors recognized his gifts. They sent him for further studies in Rome, where he earned two doctorates, in philosophy and theology, at premier universities.

He was preoccupied with the mystery of the Blessed Virgin Mary, especially in her title "the Immaculate Conception."

While he was in Rome, and even before he was ordained, he founded the Militia Immaculata, or Knights of Mary Immaculate, an organization dedicated to the pursuit of personal sanctity and characteristically Kolbean high-energy evangelization.

Also in Rome, he contracted tuberculosis, a disease for which there was no cure at the time. It left him with limited functioning in his lungs, a condition that grew worse over the course of his life, and required periodic stays (sometimes for months) in a sanitarium.

Back in Poland, he succeeded in attracting many to the Militia—mostly young people and brainy people. But he dreamed of reaching many more. In some ways he hadn't changed since he told the Blessed Virgin he would have both crowns. Maximilian dreamed big. He dreamed of reaching millions of people by means of the newly emerging media technology. He saw newsstands crowded with magazines and papers, and he wished to dedicate them to Christ. He learned of the first radio broadcasts, and he began to plan his militia's assault on the airwaves.

Before very long, he and his brother Franciscans were

running large printing presses for a magazine with circulation of a million. They operated on a large tract of land they dedicated to Mary and named the "City of the Immaculate."

Yet he lived with such a high degree of detachment that he could walk away from it all when his superiors asked him to do so. Sent to Japan, a country with very few Christians, he established a new media apostolate and built a new Franciscan monastery near Nagasaki.

He wished to go next to India. But on a visit back to Poland in 1936, his superiors were alarmed by his poor health and ordered him to remain in his homeland. He returned easily to the work he had done before. And he dreamed new dreams; he hoped one day to establish a major research university dedicated to the study of mariology, the branch of theology that focuses on the Blessed Virgin Mary. To that end, he gave conferences to his friars, and he filled notebooks sketching out plans for the books he wanted to write.

In those pages we catch glimpses of the scope and depth of his understanding of Mary's place in God's plan: "A human mother is an image of our Heavenly Mother (the Immaculata), and she in turn is the image of God's own goodness, God's own heart. God's perfections, flowing from the ineffable inner life of the Trinity, repeat themselves throughout creation in numberless forms, like so many echoes. Thus it is that, starting out from creatures, our heart can rise even to the knowledge and the love of

God in the Blessed Trinity; but our heart also loves these created forms because they do come from God, are created by him, and belong entirely to him."[1]

To pursue such lines of thought, he believed, was to understand God's plan, and Mary's place in it, more perfectly; for the Blessed Virgin always points beyond herself, to God. And she herself is the human person who most truly conforms to the divine image. God did not create Mary because her perfections were lacking in the Blessed Trinity. He created her to be an immaculate image of something he had from all eternity. What is it? That is the sort of question Father Kolbe wanted to explore in his academy . . . some day.

But the Nazi occupation of Poland brought an abrupt end to his plans. The occupiers saw Father Kolbe's communications empire as an enemy of their neo-pagan propaganda. He was arrested and released. He returned to his work. He gave conferences, and he began to sketch a dogmatic theology of Mary. This is what he was working on when the Gestapo came to take him away in February of 1941.

They took him to the labor camp at Pawiak. When he arrived, a guard approached him and grabbed at his crucifix, taunting him: "Do you still believe?" When the priest answered yes, the guard struck him, and then repeated the question. And the priest repeated his answer. The guard struck him again. The two men repeated the sequence several times before the guard gave up and stalked out.

Father Kolbe's tubercular attacks worsened at Pawiak, and he could not keep up with the camp's work regime. In late May, he was assigned with hundreds of others for transport to Auschwitz, where he offered his life to save another man.

The starvation bunker, where St. Maximilian spent his last days, was the lowest circle of the Nazis' hell on earth. There, people were sealed up and left to die in a slow agony from starvation and thirst. The guards would laugh at their despair and tell them they would leave looking like dried-up tulip bulbs.

We have the testimonies of survivors who cleaned the area and carted away the bodies. From every cell, they said, they heard screams and moans—from every cell except Father Kolbe's. There, the priest led his cellmates in hymns and prayers to Christ and the Blessed Virgin. Some of them endured for two weeks, by recycling their urine. Finally, their captors tired of waiting and ordered that the remaining prisoners be killed by injection with carbolic acid. Father Kolbe was the last to go. The man who took away his body said the priest died with a serene smile on his face.

Before his second arrest, Father Kolbe had told his fellow Franciscans, "I hope that after my death nothing remains of me, and that the wind blows away my dust over the whole earth." We hear echoes of the sacrificial language used by the early martyr, St. Ignatius of Antioch, as he wrote to the Roman Church.

Father Kolbe's body was immolated with many others on August 15, the Feast of the Assumption of the Blessed Virgin Mary, in 1941. His relics were indeed the ashes borne on the winds from the crematoria at Auschwitz.

He once said: "Our knowledge of the immaculate must bring forth fruit in sacrifice." Sacrifice is what a priest does; it is his job description. How fitting that the last words we know from Father Kolbe are his statement: "I am a Catholic priest."

God found his sacrifice pleasing. Father Kolbe was beatified just thirty years after his death and canonized a saint in 1982.

PONDER IN YOUR HEART

Pope John Paul II, on his first visit back to his native Poland, made pilgrimage to Father Kolbe's death bunker and offered Mass nearby.

"This is the victory that overcomes the world, our faith" (1 John 5:4).

These words from the Letter of Saint John come to my mind and enter my heart as I find myself in this place in which a special victory was won through faith; through the faith that gives rise to love of God and of one's neighbor, the unique love, the supreme love that is ready to "lay down (one's) life for (one's) friends" (John 15:13; cf. 10:11). A victory, therefore, through love enlivened by faith to the extreme point of the final definitive witness.

This victory through faith and love was won in this place by a man whose first name is *Maximilian Mary*. Surname: Kolbe. Profession (as registered in the books of the concentration camp): Catholic priest. Vocation: a son of Saint Francis. Birth: a son of simple, hardworking devout parents, who were weavers near Lódz. By God's grace and the Church's judgment: Blessed.

The victory through faith and love was won by him in this place, which was built for the *negation of faith*—faith in God and faith in man—and to trample radically not only on love but on all signs of human dignity, of humanity. A place built on hatred and on contempt for man in the name of a crazed ideology. A place built on cruelty. On the entrance gate which still exists is placed the inscription *"Arbeit macht frei"* [Work Makes Free], which has a sardonic sound, since its meaning was radically contradicted by what took place within.

In this site of the terrible slaughter that brought death to four million people of different nations, Father Maximilian voluntarily offered himself for death in the starvation bunker for a brother, and so won a spiritual *victory like that of Christ himself*. . . .

But was Father Maximilian Kolbe the only one? Certainly he won a victory that was immediately felt by his companions in captivity and is still felt today by the Church and the world. However, there is no doubt that many other similar victories were won. I am thinking, for example, of the death in the gas chamber of a concentration camp of the Carmelite Sister Benedicta of the Cross, whose name in the world was Edith Stein, who was an illustrious pupil of Husserl and became one of the glories of contemporary German philosophy, and who was a descendant of a Jewish family living in Wrocklaw.

Where the dignity of man was so horribly trampled on, victory was won through faith and love . . .

—ST. JOHN PAUL II, *Homily at Brzezinka Concentration Camp, June 7, 1979*

17

ST. JOSEMARIA ESCRIVA,
SAINT IN THE STREET

B Y MOST PEOPLE'S STANDARDS, FATHER JOSE-maria should have felt settled in his vocation. He had been ordained a priest since March 1925, and the intervening three and a half years had been filled with satisfying priestly ministry—at a rural parish and as chaplain to a convent and school run by an order of sisters. He lived in Spain, a predominantly Catholic country with well-established Catholic institutions.

Yet he was haunted by a sense that God had chosen him for something else, something more. He prayed insistently the blind man's plea from the Gospel: "Lord, that I may see" (Luke 18:41).

At the end of September 1928 he made a silent spiritual retreat, hoping to see more clearly what God wanted.

On the second full day of the retreat, after celebrating Mass, while the bells of the nearby church were ringing, he clearly "saw" what God wanted. God wanted him to preach the universal call to holiness—sainthood—addressed to all Christians in the ordinary circumstances of their daily life: work, family, leisure, study . . . everything. His vision showed him multitudes who would respond to this divine call of their baptism.

Seeing, they say, is believing—but it's still a far cry from the realization of the call, the follow-through. How was young Father Josemaria to bring about what God had shown him? God had omitted those details. Father Josemaria had no intention of founding anything, but he was open to God's leading. He changed his prayer slightly from "Lord, that I may see" (in Latin, *Domine, ut videam*) to "Lord, that it may be" (*Domine, ut sit*). And he watched for opportunities to share the message of "the greatness of ordinary life" with anyone who seemed inclined to receive it with understanding.

Yet few people were, and fewer still were willing to agree to take it on as a way of life—holiness in the middle of the world, in the middle of the street. Moreover, most of the few who accepted his challenge did not persevere. They slipped away, he recalled years later, "like eels."

Still, God confirmed the saint's sense of vocation and showed him that the universal call to holiness was based on the baptismal reality that all Christians are children of God. Praying one day in late September 1931, Father Josemaria experienced a powerful sense of the reality of God's fatherhood and of his own sonship. He would recall: "I walked about calling him softly, 'Father!' with the certainty that it was pleasing to him."

A few weeks later, he sat in a city church trying to pray but constantly falling into distraction. So he left the church, bought a newspaper from a street vendor, and hopped onto a streetcar. There, quite suddenly, he found himself plunged into the deepest prayer. He couldn't process anything he saw in the newspaper. He had received that sense of sonship again, this time in an overpowering way. "I felt our Lord's action, bringing to my heart and my lips, with irresistible force, the tender invocation '*Abba! Pater!*' I was on the street, in a streetcar . . . I probably made that prayer out loud. I wandered through the streets of Madrid for an hour, or perhaps two. I can't say. I didn't feel time go by. People must have taken me for a madman. I was contemplating, with lights that were not my own, this astounding truth that would remain in my soul like a burning coal and never go out."[1]

This was indisputably good news, but still he found it a hard sell. The secular climate in Spain at that time was skeptical in religious matters, and the religious culture was dominated by the idea that holiness was reserved for an elite of priests and nuns. This latter attitude, known as *clericalism*, almost always brings about a backlash, *anticlericalism*. As Spain descended into civil war in the 1930s, the anti-clerical forces got the upper hand and persecuted the Church, beginning with the elite of priests and nuns but gradually extending to all Catholics who tried to practice their faith publicly.

By this time, Father Josemaria's inspiration had begun

to take form as a life suited to men and women working in the world. Those who took on the challenge—mostly young, college-aged students—agreed to live a celibate life, sharing an ordinary home life—in a typical city home or apartment. Father Josemaria's own understanding of his calling was still inchoate. In fact, he had no name for it until his spiritual director asked him in passing how "that work of God" was going. Only then did he name his way of life *Opus Dei*, which is Latin for "Work of God."

This period of time that was traumatic for Spain proved a providential testing ground for the development of Opus Dei. This new spirit showed people a way to live as Catholics in increasingly "secular"—indeed, secularist—circumstances. When people cannot attend Mass or devotions, they can still think of their daily work as an offering, their desk or anvil or stovetop as an "altar" to God, and they can still offer their work in union with the holy sacrifice of the Mass offered throughout the world. They can still rest in the sense that they are children of God, calling on the grace of their baptism, and work with cheerfulness and confidence amid the most adverse conditions.

Members of "The Work" (as it was commonly called) experienced a "unity of life." There was no dichotomy, no separation between what they did for a living and what they professed in the creed. There was a holiness that pervaded everything. St. Josemaria spoke of the "Midas touch" enjoyed by Christians. Because they had been baptized into divine life, because they had become "partakers of the divine nature" (2 Peter 1:4), Christians extended God's power and grace into the coal mines, the cornfields, the auto-body shop, the boardroom, the bedroom, the soccer field.

Catholicism should be "Here Comes Everybody" (to steal the phrase from James Joyce), and it should reach everywhere. St. Josemaria showed the modern world a powerful means of taking it to the streets. He showed Catholics how they could sanctify their ordinary work, how they could be sanctified by their ordinary work, and how they could use their work as a means for sanctifying others. We do it by offering our work as a sacrifice, but also by doing our work well, as Christ did his work well (Mark 7:37). Then our work truly becomes an act of "co-creation" with God, and it is a sign of his goodness.

Churchmen warned St. Josemaria that he was about a century ahead of his time—that the Church just wasn't ready for his message. But he persevered, moving to Rome and working (with God and everyone else) to guide Opus Dei into the right institutional form. His counselors were right: the Church's law could not, at the time, accommodate the sort of "disorganized organization" St. Josemaria envisioned. But who, back then, could predict the changes in law and culture that would come with the latter half of the twentieth century?

Over time, and within St. Josemaria's lifetime, Opus Dei's influence extended to hundreds of thousands of people, and tens of thousands would become members. The

Second Vatican Council and the revised Code of Canon Law (the Church's legal code) would make provision for a new type of institution within the Church, a "personal prelature." Unlike dioceses, which cover territories, personal prelatures cover persons who share some common objectives, regardless of where they live. This was the form Opus Dei took in 1982, seven years after St. Josemaria's death.

He died in quite ordinary circumstances. He suffered a heart attack at home and turned to face an image of Our Lady of Guadalupe while he lay dying. He was canonized a saint a mere twenty-seven years later.

Some problems are perennial. They're never really solved. They seem to come up anew, in different forms, in every generation. If you study the lives of Paul of Tarsus and Ignatius of Antioch in the first century, Irenaeus in the second, and Augustine in the fourth, and then Aquinas in the thirteenth and Therese in the nineteenth, you'll see that they all confronted Christians who had fallen into the same seductive error. They confronted Christians who had hyperspiritualized Christianity, to the point of claiming that matter doesn't matter, the world is charged with wickedness, the body is an enemy, and human flesh is unredeemable. They confronted the spirit of laziness and despair, who claims that sainthood is not for everybody, and that most of us should resign ourselves instead to a second-class Christianity—weeks of mediocrity with a bit of God on Sunday.

St. Josemaria showed us ordinary folks a way out of such thinking, a way to avoid the trap that Christians must avoid in every age. He reminded us to live with a constant sense that we are (in the words of the saint) "other Christs, Christ himself." We are flesh-and-blood children of a loving Father, an eternal Father, an all-powerful Father. We are made to be saints and nothing else.

PONDER IN YOUR HEART

St. Josemaria preached his seminal homily "Passionately Loving the World" in 1967 in an open-air Mass at a construction site of the University of Navarre—an appropriate backdrop.

Everyday life is the true setting for your lives as Christians. Your ordinary contact with God takes place where your fellow men, your yearnings, your work and your affections are. There you have your daily encounter with Christ. It is in the midst of the most material things of the earth that we must sanctify ourselves, serving God and all mankind.

I have taught this constantly, using words from Holy Scripture. The world is not evil, because it has come from God's hands, because it is His creation, because "Yahweh looked upon it and saw that it was good" (cf. Genesis 1:7ff). We ourselves, mankind, make it evil and ugly with our sins and infidelities.

Have no doubt: any kind of evasion of the honest realities of daily life is for you, men and women of the world, something opposed to the will of God.

On the contrary, you must understand now, more clearly, that God is calling you to serve him *in and from* the ordinary, material and secular activities of human life. He waits for us every day, in the laboratory, in the operating theatre, in the army barracks, in the university chair, in the factory, in the workshop, in the fields, in the home and in all the immense panorama of work. Understand this well: there is something holy, something divine, hidden in the most ordinary situations, and it is up to each one of you to discover it.

I often said to the university students and workers who were with me in the thirties that they had to know how to "materialize" their spiritual life. I wanted to keep them from the temptation, so common then and now, of living a kind of double life. On one side, an interior life, a life of relation with God; and on the other, a separate and distinct professional, social and family life, full of small earthly realities.

No! We cannot lead a double life if we want to be Christians. There is just one life, made of flesh and spirit. And it is this life which has to become, in both soul and body, holy and filled with God. We discover the invisible God in the most visible and material things.

There is no other way. Either we learn to find our Lord in ordinary, everyday life or else we shall never find Him. That is why I can tell you that our age needs to give back to matter and to the most trivial occurrences and situations their noble and original meaning. It needs to restore them to the service of the Kingdom of God, to spiritualize them, turning them into a means and an occasion for a continuous meeting with Jesus Christ. . . .

I assure you, my sons and daughters, that when a Christian carries out with love the most insignificant everyday action, that action overflows with the transcendence of God. That is why I have told you repeatedly, and hammered away once and again on the idea that the Christian vocation consists of making heroic verse out of the prose of each day. Heaven and earth seem to merge, my sons and daughters, on the horizon. But where they really meet is in your hearts, when you sanctify your everyday lives.

18

QUEEN OF ALL SAINTS, MOTHER OF THE CHURCH

EVERY PARAGRAPH AND EVERY PAGE OF THIS book has been drawing us to this chapter. As we've moved through salvation history, considering the saints one by one, we've encountered Christ-centered men and women whose lives were profoundly influenced by the mother of their Lord. It's beautiful to read their writings and see how much the Blessed Virgin was on their mind.

St. Paul spoke of her as an essential element of "the fullness of time" (see Galatians 4:4).

St. Ignatius of Antioch mentioned her repeatedly in his correspondence. For Ignatius, she was necessary for proper understanding of Jesus Christ.

St. Irenaeus spoke of her as the "New Eve," who untied the knot of the old Eve's disobedience.

St. Jerome and St. Augustine defended her honor when, for the first time, heretics began to attack the doctrines of her perpetual virginity and her sinlessness. Augustine declared that all the righteous have truly known of sin "except the Holy Virgin Mary, of whom, for the honor of the Lord, I will have no question whatever where sin is concerned."[1]

Such true devotion continues through all the lives of all the saints we have considered: Thomas, Therese, Maximilian, Josemaria. Even Moses witnessed a dim foreshadowing of the Blessed Virgin's life—in the cooperation of his sister Miriam, Our Lady's most ancient namesake.

To be close to Christ is to be close to Mary. And how could it be otherwise?

Think, for a moment, about the fact that you have been "saved." And what is your salvation?

Here's what it is: Jesus has given his life to be your own, so that you have become a partaker of the divine nature (2 Peter 1:4). He has given you his home, heaven, so that you may live in it as your home, too. He has invited you to eat from his table. He has given his Father to be your Father.

And he has given *his mother to be your mother*!

To be saved is to be given sainthood as a grace. "You were washed, you were sanctified, you were justified in the name of the Lord Jesus Christ and in the Spirit of our God" (1 Corinthians 6:11). To live most authentically—to be most truly yourself—is to correspond to that grace at every moment of every day. That's what it means to be holy.

We are called to sainthood—to live in God's household, to live in Christ, to share his banquet, to address his Father as "Our Father," and so to be children of Mary.

We cannot assemble with the Church without entering a family relation. We cannot be Jesus' brother unless

Mary is our mother. The Church is the "assembly of the firstborn" (Hebrews 12:23). She is mother of the firstborn.

The early Christians knew this, and they gloried in it. In the Gospels, Mary has one of the largest speaking parts. In spite of her lowliness, she is the star of the opening chapters of the gospels of Matthew and Luke. Her kinfolk, Elizabeth and Zechariah, appear; but their activity is directed toward Mary's activity and resolved in Mary's activity. An angel appears, but he is sent to serve Mary. Joseph says not a word in the entire New Testament but places himself at the service of Mary and the divine Child.

When John depicts the birth of Jesus symbolically in the Book of Revelation (chapter 12), once again Mary appears at the center of the drama. She is the woman who gives birth to the "male child" who is the king of all nations. Mother and son face mortal danger and flee to the wilderness, just as we see in the infancy narratives of the Gospels. In the Apocalypse, however, we learn that the earthly events are actually a manifestation of the great cosmic war between St. Michael's angelic forces and the serpent's.

The woman is there, in Revelation, for the sake of her divine son, but his presence providentially depends upon her cooperation.

The "woman" of Revelation is clearly Mary, and yet she is also the Church, the mother of "many offspring." This is not a contradiction or confusion. It's the way the biblical peoples thought and expressed themselves. "Israel" was a man, a historical figure, but it was also the name of the man's offspring and their nation. In the same way, the name David designated Israel's great king, but also his capital city, his household, and his descendants.

Thus, the early Church Fathers, having fed themselves on Scripture, could say such things as "We call the Church by the name of Mary, for she deserves a double name."[2] So said St. Ephrem of Syria in the fourth century; and the man practiced what he preached, adding that Jesus had "entrusted Mary, his Church"[3] to John the Beloved Disciple. Nor was this a peculiarity of Syriac culture. In the same century, St. Ambrose of Milan taught that Mary, as virgin and mother, "prefigures the Church which is undefiled [cf. Ephesians 5:27] yet wed. A Virgin conceived us of the Spirit, a Virgin brings us forth without travail."[4]

A little bit later, St. Augustine developed this typology still further: "How is it that you do not belong to the Virgin's birth, if you are members of Christ? Mary gave birth to our Head; the Church gave birth to you. Indeed the Church also is both virgin and mother—mother, because of her womb of charity; virgin, because of the integrity of her faith and piety. She gives birth to peoples, but her members belong to the One only of whom she herself is the body and the spouse. In this, too, she bears the likeness of that other Virgin, the fact that she is also the mother of unity among many."[5]

Much earlier, St. Irenaeus had used the same imagery in a poetic way, when he described Jesus as "the pure One opening purely that pure womb which regenerates men unto God, and which he himself made pure."[6] Remember, please, that St. Irenaeus was the disciple of St. Polycarp, who was the disciple of St. John the Apostle, to whom Jesus had entrusted the Blessed Virgin.

This is the Church's perennial doctrine of Mary, drawn from the Book of Revelation and also from the Acts of the Apostles (1:14), where the disciples are gathered around the Virgin Mother on the vigil of the Church's birth. Mary indeed possesses great privileges, but she has received them all from the pure One, the Son of God, the Eternal Word, Jesus, whom she bore in her womb.

God gave her singular graces because of her unique role in history. He made her sinless from the moment of her conception. He called her to be "Ever-Virgin."

Why? Because she was to become the vessel of God's presence in the world! Now, the vessels used in the temple service were made, by God's command, of the purest, most precious metals; and they were reserved only for sacred use. You could not repurpose the temple's golden altar as an end table. You could not take the chalice used for libations and fill it with a cold beer on a hot summer night. Apart from the temple service, even the finest wine would profane the sacred vessels. It's not that there's anything wrong with end tables or alcoholic beverages, but the temple vessels were sacred and for God's use only.

Mary's body was that kind of vessel. Once blessed with

God's presence, she could not simply "retire" and resume an ordinary married life. What would be permissible and even honorable for others would be a profanation for the Mother of God. And it should go without saying that God would preserve the vessel of his presence from contamination by sin.

Mary is a member of the Church. Yet she is Mother of the Church. She is a saint. Yet she is Queen of All Saints. If—as St. Jerome showed us in Chapter 12 and St. Augustine in Chapter 13—the martyrs wield great power from heaven, how much more will God give to the woman who is Queen of Martyrs, whose soul was pierced by a sword (Luke 2:35) as she suffered alongside her Son?

He already bestowed power on her when she was a lowly, unknown girl from a backwater village, when she was living in a cave cut out of the hillside. God arranged events so that all of history turned on her answer to an angel's invitation. That's greater power than any earthly king ever possessed. Imagine what God has given her now that she has triumphed with her Son—now that she is clothed with the sun and crowned with the stars (Revelation 12:1).

Such is Mary's dignity—and she shares it with all the saints, with all her children in the Church. Christ merited her power to merit, and he invited us to engage with him in his meritorious work. This is what saints do. As St. Paul put it, they "complete what is lacking in Christ's afflictions for the sake of his body, that is, the Church" (Colossians

1:24). The saints are "God's co-workers" (1 Corinthians 3:9), because God wills them to be so. God wills us to be so.

And Mary is the great sign that we can do it. We can cooperate with God. We can correspond to his grace. Jesus was right: we can be perfect as his heavenly Father is perfect (Matthew 5:48).

The Blessed Virgin Mary is not only the end point of this book, but the end point of the Church. She is already what we are ever striving to be. She is an icon of the heavenly Church, with which the earthly Church has union. There are not two churches, but one Church, and she embodies it already in heaven.

Her name should be the last word in any consideration of sainthood, for she is Queen of All Saints and Mother of the Church. She is Our Lady and Our Mother: Mary. Scriptures show!

PONDER IN YOUR HEART

The Second Vatican Council spoke of Mary's God-given role in the Church.

There is but one Mediator as we know from the words of the apostle, "for there is one God and one mediator of God and men, the man Christ Jesus, who gave himself a redemption for all" (1 Timothy

2:5–6). The maternal duty of Mary toward men in no wise obscures or diminishes this unique mediation of Christ, but rather shows his power. For all the salvific influence of the Blessed Virgin on men originates, not from some inner necessity, but from the divine pleasure. It flows forth from the super-abundance of the merits of Christ, rests on his mediation, depends entirely on it and draws all its power from it. In no way does it impede, but rather does it foster the immediate union of the faithful with Christ.

Predestined from eternity by that decree of divine providence which determined the incarnation of the Word to be the Mother of God, the Blessed Virgin was in this earth the virgin Mother of the Redeemer, and above all others and in a singular way the generous associate and humble handmaid of the Lord. She conceived, brought forth and nourished Christ. She presented him to the Father in the temple, and was united with him by compassion as he died on the Cross. In this singular way she cooperated by her obedience, faith, hope and burning charity in the work of the Savior in giving back supernatural life to souls. Wherefore she is our mother in the order of grace.

This maternity of Mary in the order of grace began with the consent which she gave in faith at the Annunciation and which she sustained without wavering beneath the cross, and lasts until the eternal fulfillment of all the elect. Taken up to heaven she did not lay aside this salvific duty, but by her constant intercession continued to bring us the gifts of eternal salvation. By her maternal charity, she cares for the brethren of her Son, who still journey on earth surrounded by dangers and difficulties, until they are led into the happiness of their true home. Therefore the Blessed Virgin is invoked by the Church under the titles of Advocate, Auxiliatrix, Adjutrix, and Mediatrix. This, however, is to be so understood that it neither takes away from nor adds anything to the dignity and efficaciousness of Christ the one Mediator.

For no creature could ever be counted as equal with the Incarnate Word and Redeemer. Just as the priesthood of Christ is shared in various ways both by the ministers and by the faithful, and as the one goodness of God is really communicated in different ways to his creatures, so also the unique mediation of the Redeemer does not exclude but rather gives rise to a manifold cooperation which is but a sharing in this one source.

The Church does not hesitate to profess this subordinate role of Mary. It knows it through unfailing experience of it and commends it to the hearts of the faithful, so that encouraged by this maternal help they may the more intimately adhere to the Mediator and Redeemer.[7]

—SECOND VATICAN COUNCIL, *Lumen Gentium: The Dogmatic Constitution on the Church*

LAST WORDS

FAMILY FIRST

Let's go back, for a moment, to Assisi.

Like so many other pilgrims down the centuries, I experienced a breakthrough there—though not in any of the sites famous for their holiness or beauty. I met the saints—or perhaps I should say they met me—in a nondescript, secular, institutional setting, in the midst of a family crisis. And that is probably as it should be.

By then I had been a Catholic for more than a decade. On Easter Vigil in 1986 I repeated the standard pledge of those who come into full communion with the Church: "I believe and profess all that the holy Catholic Church teaches, believes, and proclaims to be revealed by God." And I meant it. Afterward, when I recited the creed on Sundays and affirmed my faith "in the Communion of Saints," I held nothing back, and I could probably have taught an advanced theology course on the subject and edified a classroom full of my best students.

But the doctrine hadn't yet traveled the whole way from my head to my heart. When I stepped off our tour bus in that little Italian town, I held what Blessed John Henry Newman called "notional assent," which is a very good thing. It means that we accept a doctrine on principle, on abstract and intellectual terms.

By the time I left the hospital in Assisi, however, I possessed what Newman called "real assent." I knew the saints not as a proposition, but as my closest kin.

The analogy is rather exact. When I was preparing for marriage, I knew that my fiancée's family would soon become my in-laws. Though we had no resemblance at the level of our DNA, we would forever afterward be *family* to one another. I remember showing up for a Kirk family gathering shortly before our wedding; there I met the entire cast of characters from Kimberly's reminiscences of her childhood. There, in her parents' living room, were siblings and their spouses and children, aunts and uncles, close cousins and distant cousins—a crowd with the most amazing array of virtues, styles, gifts, and eccentricities. And they were all so different from my own family back home. I remember coming to the sudden realization that *all these men, women, and children would soon be my family.* My family was growing much larger—and, with the children and grandchildren Kimberly and I planned to have together, it would (we hoped) grow larger and larger still.

It was a beautiful realization, and it moved me deeply. Yet all that sudden infusion of familial fellowship was still minuscule compared to the family God gave me in 1986—and showed me years later in Assisi.

In Assisi, it was as if the walls had blown off our home with a gust of the Holy Spirit, and I could see for the first time that my clan was vaster than I had ever imagined. It contained multitudes. Yet there were no distant cousins, only brothers and sisters in Christ.

In his classic discussion of assent, Blessed Newman wrote, "the heart is commonly reached, not through the reason, but through the imagination, by means of direct impressions, by the testimony of facts and events, by history, by description. Persons influence us, voices melt us, looks subdue us, deeds inflame us."

Persons, voices, looks, and deeds—that's the stuff of family life. The Communion of Saints is a family first of all. In Assisi I came to know my true family's active presence, and I came to own this fundamental Christian doctrine. To "believe in the Communion of Saints" is not simply a matter of affirming the immortality of the soul and whatever consequences happen to come with it. It is, rather, coming to terms with the reality of life in a true home: God's home.

To be in God's family: that is the deepest meaning of *sainthood*, and it's the deepest meaning of *salvation*. For the two words are functional equivalents. Only saints are saved; and only the saved are saints.

Sainthood does not mean sinlessness. It means, however, that we're working on the problem, and in a serious way. Pope Francis began his pontificate by urging: "Never forget this: The Lord never gets tired of forgiving us. It is we who get tired of asking for forgiveness." As Blessed Mother Teresa of Calcutta often said, saints are sinners who never give up.

Salvation is neither otherworldly nor this-worldly. It's holy.

Through the lives of the saints—through *our* lives—holiness touches upon all the things of the earth. "Behold," Jesus said, "I make *all* things new" (Revelation 21:5). He does this through our touch—yours and mine—through the touch of the saints who live in him—the saints who live in communion.

BIBLIOGRAPHY

For a sampling of recent studies on angels and saints from a wide range of biblical, historical, and theological perspectives, see the following:

Mother Alexandra, *The Holy Angels* (Petersham, MA: St. Bede's, 1987).

H. George Anderson, J. Francis Stafford, Joseph A. Burgess (eds.), *The One Mediator, the Saints, and Mary: Lutherans and Catholics in Dialogue VIII* (Minneapolis: Augsburg, 1992).

Mike Aquilina, *Angels of God: The Bible, the Church, and the Heavenly Hosts* (Cincinnati: Servant, 2009).

Andrew J. Bandstra, *In The Company of Angels* (Grand Rapids, MI: CRC Publications, 1995).

Margaret Barker, *An Extraordinary Gathering of Angels* (London: MQ Publications, 2004).

Matthew Bunson, Margaret Bunson, Stephen Bunson, *Encyclopedia of Saints* (Huntington, IN: Our Sunday Visitor, 2003).

Patrick Madrid, *Any Friend of God's Is a Friend of Mine: A Biblical and Historical Exploration of the Catholic Doctrine of the Communion of Saints* (San Diego, CA: Basilica, 1996).

BIBLIOGRAPHY

David Matzko McCarthy, *Sharing God's Good Company: A Theology of the Communion of Saints* (Grand Rapids, MI: Eerdmans, 2012).

Ellen Muehlberger, *Angels in Late Ancient Christianity* (New York: Oxford University Press, 2013).

Marcel Poorthuis and J. Schwartz (eds.), *Saints and Role Models in Judaism and Christianity* (Boston: E.J. Brill, 2004).

Jon M. Sweeney, *The Lure of Saints: A Protestant Experience of Catholic Tradition* (Brewster, MA: Paraclete Press, 2005).

NOTES

A NOTE ON MY SOURCES: I've drawn texts of the early Church Fathers from three nineteenth-century series: the Ante-Nicene Fathers (abbreviated ANF); the Nicene and Post-Nicene Fathers, Series 1 (NPNF1); and the Nicene and Post-Nicene Fathers, Series 2 (NPNF2). I've chosen these series because they're easily accessible online. My citations are simple: NPNF2 1:1 means Nicene and Post-Nicene Fathers, Series 2, volume 1, page 1. I've taken the liberty of updating the language from these old translations.

2: THE ONLY SAINT

1. Joshua Berman, *The Temple: Its Symbolism and Meaning Then and Now* (Northvale, NJ: Jason Aronson, 1995), 1–12.
2. St. Ignatius of Antioch, *Letter to the Ephesians* 9.2.

3: FOR *ALL* THE SAINTS

1. John Henry Cardinal Newman, "The Individuality of the Soul," in *Parochial and Plain Sermons*, vol. 4 (London: Longmans, Green, 1909), 80–81, 83–84.

4: WHAT DO SAINTS DO?

1. *Lumen Gentium* 8.49.

6: A GATHERING OF ANGELS

1. St. Augustine, *City of God* 12.1.

7: ST. MICHAEL AND THE ANGELS

1. St. Ambrose of Milan, *Letters* (Oxford, UK: James Parker, 1881), 146–147.

8: HOLY MOSES

1. *Babylonian Talmud: Tractate Nedarim* 38a.
2. *Babylonian Talmud: Tractate Yebamoth* 49b.
3. *Babylonian Talmud, Tractate Sanhedrin* 98b.
4. St. Cyril of Jerusalem, *Catechetical Lectures* 10.7, NPNF2 7:59.

9: ST. PAUL, SON OF GOD

1. St. John Chrysostom, *Homilies on Ephesians* 1.1, NPNF1 13:50.

10: ST. IGNATIUS OF ANTIOCH, GOD'S WHEAT

1. St. Ignatius of Antioch, *Letter to the Ephesians* 7, ANF 1:52.
2. St. Ignatius of Antioch, *Letter to the Polycarp* 3, ANF 1:94.
3. St. Ignatius of Antioch, *Letter to the Magnesians* 9, ANF 1:62.
4. St. Ignatius of Antioch, *Letter to the Smyrnaeans* 8, ANF 1:90.
5. St. Ignatius of Antioch, *Letter to the Philadelphians* 4, ANF 1:81.
6. St. Ignatius of Antioch, *Letter to the Smyrnaeans* 7, ANF 1:89
7. St. Ignatius of Antioch, *Letter to the Magnesians* 6, ANF 1:61.

8. St. Ignatius of Antioch, *Letter to the Romans,* prologue, ANF 1:73.

9. St. Ignatius of Antioch, *Letter to the Romans* 2, 4, 7, ANF 1:74–77.

11: ST. IRENAEUS OF LYONS, BLESSED PEACEMAKER

1. Recorded in Eusebius of Caesarea, *Church History* 5.24, NPNF2 1:244.

2. St. Polycarp of Smyrna, *Letter to the Philippians* 7, ANF 1:34.

3. St. Irenaeus of Lyons, *Against the Heresies* 4.13.4, ANF 1:478.

4. St. Irenaeus of Lyons, *Against the Heresies* 4.9.1, ANF 1:472.

5. St. Irenaeus of Lyons, *Against the Heresies* 1.10.3, ANF 1:331.

6. St. Irenaeus of Lyons, *Against the Heresies* 4.18.5, ANF 1:486.

7. St. Irenaeus of Lyons, *Against the Heresies* 1.10.3, ANF 1:331–332.

8. St. Irenaeus of Lyons, *Against the Heresies* 3.3.1–3. Translated by Dominic J. Unger, OFM Cap., in "St. Irenaeus and the Roman Primacy," *Theological Studies,* September 1952, 364–365.

12: ST. JEROME AND HIS CIRCLE

1. *Preface to the Commentary on Isaiah* 1.

2. St. Jerome, *Letters* 27.2, NPNF2 6:44.

3. St. Jerome, *Against Vigiliantius* 6–8, NPNF2 6:419–421.

NOTES

14: ST. THOMAS AQUINAS,
BIBLICAL THEOLOGIAN

1. Bernard Gui, "Life of St. Thomas Aquinas," in Kenelm Foster, OP, *The Life of St. Thomas Aquinas: Biographical Documents* (Baltimore: Helicon, 1959), 39.

15: ST. THERESE OF LISIEUX,
SAINT OF LITTLE THINGS

1. St. Therese of Lisieux, *The Story of a Soul* (London: Burns, Oates, and Washbourne, 1912). Retrieved from www.gutenberg.org on March 31, 2011. I have adapted the language slightly to conform to U.S. English.
2. Letters appended to St. Therese of Lisieux, *The Story of a Soul* (London: Burns, Oates, and Washbourne, 1912). Retrieved from www.gutenberg.org on March 31, 2011.

16: ST. MAXIMILIAN KOLBE,
SAINT OF AUSCHWITZ

1. Quoted in H. M. Manteau-Bonamy, *Immaculate Conception and the Holy Spirit: The Marian Teachings of Father Kolbe* (Kenosha, WI: Prow, 1977), 23.

17: ST. JOSEMARIA ESCRIVA,
SAINT IN THE STREET

1. John Coverdale, *Uncommon Faith: The Early Years of Opus Dei, 1928–1943* (Princeton, NJ: Scepter, 2002), 93.

18: QUEEN OF ALL SAINTS,
MOTHER OF THE CHURCH

1. St. Augustine of Hippo, *On Nature and Grace* 36.

2. St. Ephrem of Syria, "Sermon for the night of the Resurrection," quoted in Luigi Gambero, *Mary and the Fathers of the Church: The Blessed Virgin Mary in Patristic Thought* (San Francisco: Ignatius Press, 1999), 115.

3. Ibid.

4. St. Ambrose of Milan, *Exposition of the Holy Gospel According to Saint Luke* 2.7 (Etna, CA: CTOS, 2003), 44.

5. St. Augustine, *Sermons* 192.2.

6. St. Irenaeus of Lyons, *Against the Heresies* 4.33.11, ANF 1:509.

7. Second Vatican Council, *Lumen Gentium: The Dogmatic Constitution on the Church*, nn. 60–62, Nov. 21, 1964. Retrieved from www.vatican.va on April 4, 2011.